Schindler's Krakow

Schindler's Krakow

The City Under the Nazis

Andrew Rawson

Pen & Sword
MILITARY

First published in Great Britain by
PEN AND SWORD MILITARY
an imprint of
Pen and Sword Books Ltd
47 Church Street
Barnsley
South Yorkshire S70 2AS

ISBN 978 1 47382 797 4

Printed and bound in England by
CPI Group (UK) Ltd, Croydon, CR0 4YY

Typeset in Times by CHIC GRAPHICS

Pen & Sword Books Ltd incorporates the imprints of
Pen & Sword Books Ltd incorporates the imprints of Pen & Sword
Archaeology, Atlas, Aviation, Battleground, Discovery,
Family History, History, Maritime, Military, Naval, Politics,
Railways, Select, Social History, Transport, True Crime,
Claymore Press, Frontline Books, Leo Cooper, Praetorian Press,
Remember When, Seaforth Publishing and Wharncliffe.

For a complete list of Pen and Sword titles please contact
Pen and Sword Books Limited
47 Church Street, Barnsley, South Yorkshire, S70 2AS, England
E-mail: enquiries@pen-and-sword.co.uk
Website: www.pen-and-sword.co.uk

Contents

Introduction

Hans Frank's General Government ruled Krakow with an iron fist between September 1939 and January 1945. They forcibly moved people, eradicated their history and culture and then arrested and executed many. The Jews were soon confined to Podgórze ghetto where they were put to work in factories such as Oskar Schindler's. There followed deportations and the bloody liquidation of the ghetto as the Jews were moved into Plaszow concentration camp. Selections and murders followed but Schindler bribed and conned his way to save his workforce before moving them to his Sudetenland home town. The Polish underground did what they could to fight back until the Soviets reached the city.

Thomas Keneally's 1982 book *Schindler's Ark* and Steven Spielberg's 1993 film *Schindler's List* brought parts of Krakow's wartime story to the world's attention; this book explores the complete story. If you have read the book or seen the film, you will recognize many stories. If you have not, make sure you do; they will add to your knowledge and experience.

Also in this book are instructions on how to explore Schindler's Krakow, a city of contrasts with a medieval centre and communist era outskirts. There is information about the museums, including Wawel Castle, Schindler's Factory, the Gestapo Museum and the Home Army Museum as well as advice on how to find your way around the Podgórze Ghetto and Plaszow concentration camp. The city is also a base for visiting Auschwitz-Birkenau. The companion volume, Auschwitz, the Nazi Solution, is an illustrated history and guide to the extermination camp.

Chapter 1

The Battle for Poland

Preparing for War

Poland had concentrated on the Soviet threat throughout the 1930s, building fortifications on its eastern borders under *Plan S*, but spent 1938 watching anxiously as Nazi Germany expanded the boundaries of the Third Reich. It began with the Union with Austria (the *Anschluss*) in March 1938 and then the political stand-off at the Munich conference in September 1938, which resulted in Germany annexing the German speaking Sudetenland region of Czechoslovakia. Poland also occupied a small area adjacent to Lower Silesia while Hungary took more Slovakian territory. German Minister of Foreign Affairs, Joachim von Ribbentrop, also demanded the Free City of Danzig on the Baltic coast be incorporated into the Reich.

The rest of the Czech region was occupied in March 1939 and the people of Poland would have heard of the brutal repressions in the new Protectorate of Bohemia and Moravia. The Lithuanian territory of Memel was also handed over to Nazi Germany.

Commander-in-Chief of the Polish armed forces, *Marszalek* Edward Rydz-Smigly, had to protect the country's western border against the *Wehrmacht* and the *Luftwaffe*. Although the military solution was to defend river lines, it would have left the Germans free to occupy the western districts of Pomerania, Greater Poland

Marshal Rydz-Smigly.

and Upper Silesia, where many industries were based. So he issued plans for Plan West (*Plan Zachod*) towards the end of March 1939 in which the Polish Army (*Wojsko Polskie*) would form five army groups (Modlin, Pomorze, Poznan, Lódź and Krakow) along the border; the Autonomous Operational Group would be their reserve.

The Invasion Begins

The Wehrmacht crossed the Polish border at dawn on 1 September as the Luftwaffe's planes filled the skies. Sixty Heinkel He111 bombers led Junkers Ju87 Stuka dive bombers and Dornier Do17 bombers, towards the airfields around Krakow. While Balice airfield (now John Paul II International Airport), west of the city, saw the bombers first, they flew past and over the city. They bombed Czyzyny airfield but only hit training aircraft because the fighters had been moved to temporary airfields.

Polskie Radio broadcast the following announcement at 6.30 am:

> *"So it is a war! As of today, all matters and issues are pushed to the back. We are now switching our whole public and private lives to special tracks. We have entered the time*

Stuka dive bombers search for targets.

of war. The efforts of the whole nation must go in one direction. We are all soldiers now. There is only one thing on our minds now: to fight until we win."

But the Polish air force only had 44 combat planes while the Luftwaffe had 749. It meant the German bombers could hit targets across Krakow, particularly the railway station and freight depot, without interference. All the people could do was huddle in their air-raid shelters and hope the German planes did not drop gas bombs.

General Broni (Lieutenant General) Antoni Szylling's Krakow Army was stretched from Czestochowa in the north, through the fortified Silesia area (Slask), to Bielsko in the south and then along the Czech border as far east as Czorsztyn. He only had a few infantry divisions, two cavalry brigades and thirty-five light tanks to hold the line. *Generalleutnant* Wilhelm List's Fourteenth Army had four Panzer divisions armed with 800 tanks and armoured cars.

By the end of the first day, the Panzer divisions were threatening both flanks of the Krakow Army while the Luftwaffe was wreaking havoc on its lines of communication. Szylling's centre was holding and Fourteenth Army had been stopped south-east of the city. But *Generalleutnant* Walther von Reichenau's Tenth Army was advancing to the Vistula far behind his north flank.

The Krakow Army Withdraws
The breakthrough compromised the Krakow Army's position and Marshal Rydz-Smigly gave Szylling permission to withdraw from Silesia, to the surprise of Generals Jan Jagmin-Sadowski and Mieczyslaw Boruta. After abandoning their fortified positions, Operational Group Jagmin (previously OG Slask) fell back along the north bank of the Vistula while Operational Group Boruta (previously OG Bielsko) followed the south bank.

General Jagmin-Sadowski wanted to hold Krakow's forts and counter-attack but Rydz-Smigly had to consider the strategic plan. His southern flank would disintegrate if part of his army was cut off and forced to surrender. All Generals Jagmin and Boruta could do was order their men to deploy to the east of Krakow, knowing that they were being chased by a mechanized enemy. The long march east under air attack was bad for morale and abandoning Krakow, where many of their families lived, only made it fall lower.

News that Great Britain and France had declared war on Germany on 3 September prompted the French diplomats to leave Krakow. The city authority's staff followed, including City Mayor Boleslaw Czuchajowski and Province Governor Jozef Tyminski. They left Deputy Mayor Stanislaw Klimecki and his assistant, Dr Wincenty Bogdanowski, to run a new Citizens' Committee. The police also left, leaving the citizens' guard to guard military and municipal property.

The Royal Castle's staff spent the evening of 3 September packing treasures and archives into crates on Wawel Hill. They were loaded onto boats and were taken down the River Vistula into Romania en route for France; they eventually ended up in the United States.

Rydz-Smigly's headquarters staff left Krakow on 4 September and the last Polish Army units moved out the following night. Early the following morning German motorcycle patrols drove along the quiet streets as the people watched anxiously, waiting to see what happened next. Colonel Pfau accepted control of Krakow on behalf of the Wehrmacht while German army units seized key buildings across the city. A headquarters was set up in the Royal Castle on Wawel Hill and immediately took twenty-five members of the Citizens' Committee hostage, to make sure no one interfered with the occupation. They were released at midnight once the city was secure; it had fallen without a shot being fired.

The Surrender of Poland

While the people of Krakow came to terms with the occupation, the Polish Army was fighting on to the east. Marshal Rydz-Smigly wanted to withdraw his remaining troops to the Romanian bridgehead, where south-east Poland bordered Romania (now in the Ukraine). But the Krakow Army was struggling to keep ahead of the Wehrmacht's Panzers and was nearly surrounded west of the Dunajec

German Panzer IV tanks on the move.

and Nida rivers. OG Jagmin and OG Boruta faced a tough fight along the Vistula and they were regrouped on the east bank of the river San.

But the Krakow Army then found Panzer divisions had encircled the Lublin area, blocking its route to the Romanian bridgehead. General Tadeusz Piskor organized an attack on Tomaszow Lubelski, to break through the German lines, on 17 September but his troops heard bad news the following day. German megaphones announced the departure of the Polish government and the Commander-in-Chief while the Red Army had crossed Poland's eastern border. While Piskor's men fought on, they could not break out and on 19 September he ordered one final attack later that night. The attempt failed and he was forced to surrender his command, including a large part of the Krakow Army.

While the fight in the south was over, the siege of Warsaw continued until ammunition, food and water ran out on 28 September. The last battle in the campaign for Poland came to an end on 5 September at Kock, eighty miles south-east of the capital.

Around 63,000 Polish soldiers had been killed and nearly

138,000 wounded. Over 400,000 had been captured by the Wehrmacht and another 230,000 by the Red Army; only 80,000 had escaped into Romania and Hungary. The people of Poland were completely shocked by the rapid demise of their armed forces and they blamed the generals for letting them down. Some believed Great Britain and France had betrayed their country for not coming to their aid. Only after hearing of the capitulation of the Netherlands, Belgium and France in May and June 1940 did they see that no army was a match for the German *Blitzkrieg*.

The Refugees' Story
While that is the story of the Polish armed forces, hundreds of thousands of Polish civilians were also affected by the German and Soviet invasion. The people of Poland had been worried about the German threats, in particular young men and women who feared they would be deported as forced labour. Many families went to stay with relatives in the country, some sent their children away and others obtained emigration papers. More left when the air raids began on 1 September.

Mayor Klimecki's promises that services would continue as normal were kept as the trams kept running and the gas, water and electricity stayed on. But his appeals for calm were ignored as the streets came alive with people. Many were Silesian refugees and they were full of bad news about the situation at the front. Bishop Adam Sapieha organized the Citizens' Aid Committee to help feed and house as many as possible.

On day three of the war, a Sunday morning, panic swept across Krakow as Polish troops started withdrawing. Many Krakovians left their homes and while a few founds seats on a train, the rest headed east on foot, pushing carts and prams full of belongings. They faced a difficult journey, walking alongside the retreating Polish Army units, as the Luftwaffe's planes flew overhead looking for targets.

Many went to stay with friends and family in Lviv (Lwow), unaware it would soon fall under Soviet rule. Many professors were evacuated to the Jan Kazimierz University in Lviv, while fleeing students were given accommodation there. Others who knew they

Refugees on the road.

would be targeted by the Nazis because of their beliefs headed for Romania and Hungary.

Many refugees were motivated to continue walking east but others decided to head for home. Some turned back, defeated by a lack of money, failing stamina, or to save their families further hardships. The Soviet invasion of Poland's eastern territories on 17 September forced many more to have a change of heart and go home. Around 12,000 refugees had walked back to Krakow by the end of October, some having escaped from the Soviet held area.

The return home was not a happy one for many, particularly the Jews, because they had to come to terms with the curfew and new strict laws imposed by the General Government; some found their houses had been looted. They also found a city overcrowded by people who had left their villages, believing it would be easier to find work in the city; they were wrong.

Many of those who escaped east found themselves in Soviet controlled territory by the end of September and unable to return. They had illegal immigration status and many were arrested and deported to labour camps across the Soviet Union.

On 30 July 1941 Polish Prime Minister, Wladyslaw Sikorski, and Soviet Ambassador to Great Britain, Ivan Mayski, signed an agreement which gave the Poles their freedom and many headed to Moscow where the Polish embassy provided assistance. Thousands of men joined General Wladyslaw Anders' new Polish Army hoping to fight alongside the Red Army, but political differences, logistical problems and the threat of typhus forced the Poles to leave the Soviet Union with their families. They faced an epic journey across Iran, Iraq and Palestine before fighting in the Italian campaign. They played a major role in the Battle for Monte Cassino, capturing the monastery on 18 May 1944.

Chapter 2

Taking Control of Krakow

The *Einsatzgruppen* Move In

Germany had been planning its attack on Polish society since May 1939. Operation Tannenberg had compiled the names of 61,000 activists, professors, teachers, actors and former army officers. Germans living in Poland also helped to prepare the lists and 2,000 Polish were rounded up in Germany.

German troops had entered Krakow at dawn on 6 September 1939 and posters announcing the new regime's rules immediately appeared across the city. A curfew confined everyone to their homes from 6.30pm until 5am and state and city officials were given two days' notice to return to work. Everyone had to hand in any weapons, ammunition or explosives they were holding or face imprisonment and possible execution.

A short distance behind the first troops came the dreaded *Einsatzgruppe I*. Five Special Operational Groups (*Einsatzgruppen*) were formed with officers from the Gestapo, the security police and the criminal police in August 1939. They were ready to carry out the Polish part of Operation Tannenberg. *SS-Brigadeführer* Bruno Streckenbach arrived in Krakow on 6 September 1939 and *Einsatzgruppe I* took over the police station at 21 Siemiradzkiego St, in the north-west suburbs. Two days later his men set about identifying and marking all Jewish businesses, restaurants and shops with the Star of David, exposing their owners to abuse.

Streckenbach had four Special Units (*Einsatzkommandos*) under his command and they had orders to *"to counter all elements hostile to the German Reich at the rear of the fighting army"*. *Einsatzkommando*

2/1 occupied Silesian House (Dom Slaski) at 2 Pomorska St and immediately set to work arresting, interrogating and executing the people on its lists. They were probably helped by members of the German Peoples' Self Protection paramilitary group (*Volksdeutscher Selbstschutz*) whose members were ethnic Germans living in the city.

When men were accused of stealing near Plaszow railway station on Sunday 10 September 1939, a shot was fired as they were arrested. *Einsatzkommandos* cordoned off the area and raided nearby apartments, looking for names on their lists. Some were beaten, a grenade was thrown into a cellar and thirteen men were arrested. They were frog-marched to the Jewish cemetery on Jerozolimska and shot.

Two days later allegations were made that shots had been fired at Luftwaffe planes from the Podgórze district; ten Jews were taken from nearby apartments and shot in the street. The same day thirty-two people were dragged from their homes on Grodzka, in the city centre, taken to St Michael's prison and executed. News of the shootings spread quickly across the city, as the Germans hoped. They were shot in public to make the people of Krakow think twice about engaging in sabotage or resistance activities.

The Terror Begins
The General Government soon started introducing new decrees, changing everyone's daily lives. The Reichsmark replaced the Polish zloty as the new currency and the amount people could change at a time was limited. Shops had to remain open from 9am to 5.30pm and owners were banned from hoarding items or raising prices. Shoppers were not allowed to panic buy and the penalty for stealing was death. Then on 19 September a most unpopular decree was introduced when bars and shops were banned from selling Poland's favourite drink, vodka. Beer could still be sold but servicemen had to be served first and the locals could share what little was left.

The Nazi decrees affected all aspects of life. The speed limit on the busy streets was reduced to 10 km/hour while pedestrians were not allowed to stop on pavements and had to walk on the left. Although the new decrees made life difficult, they were mild

Raising the Governor-General's flag above Wawel Castle.

compared to what was to come. Announcements about attacks on German citizens and acts of sabotage were made on 20 September and arrests and executions followed.

The Krakow Municipal Board called for a halt to acts of violence when two soldiers were killed and Mayor Stanislaw Klimecki was held hostage, to safeguard against further murders. Civilians were banned from entering the city parks at any time and from Planty Park, the green belt surrounding the old town, after dark; trespassers would be shot on sight.

Attacks on the Jews

On 8 September 1939 Mayor Klimecki asked the Jewish social activist Marek Biberstein to organize a provisional Jewish council. No one wanted to join so *SS-Oberscharführer* Paul Siebert, in his capacity as head of the Gestapo section dealing with religious groups, gave Biberstein an ultimatum. He had 48 hours to form a twelve-person Jewish Council (*Judenrat*) and he was to be president.

The General Government's first order to the Judenrat was to impose a new tax on everyone with Jewish heritage going back four generations. A census would be held to make sure they all paid; all 68,000 of them. They were also not allowed to store, sell or give away their property, because the Germans intended to confiscate it. Another instruction called for the confiscation of religious treasures and historical artefacts from the city's synagogues. Many Jews were then put to work filling in air-raid trenches. German soldiers also picked out orthodox Jews for verbal and physical abuse and on the third day of occupation all Jewish cafés, shops and firms were made to display the Star of David. It meant they could be harassed at will.

While the Jews were singled out for unfair treatment, the Poles hoped the Germans would be fair towards them; but they would not. The police refused to acknowledge crimes against Poles or Jews but they handed out harsh punishments if a German was a victim. For example, on 20 September a group of Polish hostages, including Krakow's President, Stanislaw Klimecki, were imprisoned following the alleged assault of a German soldier.

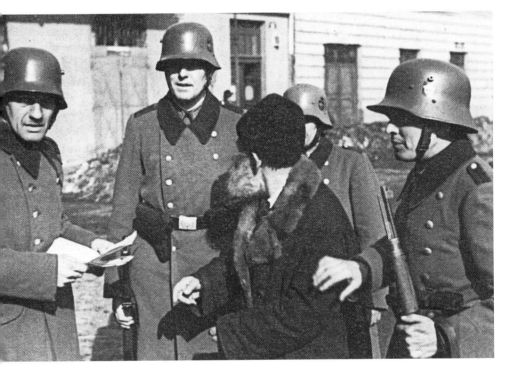

German soldiers hassle an elderly Jew.

Closing the University

Academics met in Krakow's famous Jagiellonian University on 9 September 1939 to organize a Provisional School Commission and put in place a city-wide plan to maintain a functioning education system. But teachers had been called up by the armed services, many children had been evacuated and school buildings had been occupied by the Wehrmacht. Even so, the Commission had set up many primary and secondary classes before it was banned at the end of the month.

On 19 October the university senate announced that students could start enrolling at Jagiellonian University. On 3 November Professor Tadeusz Lehr-Splawinski, announced that classes would begin in three days. The Rector immediately received a letter from *SS-Obersturmbannführer* Bruno Müller, head of the local Einsatzkommando, telling him to gather the professors on the opening day because he wanted to explain the National Socialist approach to education.

The professors gathered as instructed, only to see armed guards follow Müller into the lecture theatre. He explained that the Security Service saw the university as a hotbed of anti-German attitudes and then stated that classes had been started without the General Government's consent. They were then told they were under arrest as part of Special Action Krakow (*Sonderaktion Krakau*).

The professors were escorted out of the lecture theatre, manhandled onto lorries and driven to Montelupich prison. They were soon moved to Mazowiecka Barracks and then taken by train to Wroclaw prison, 150 miles to the north-west, en-route to Sachsenhausen concentration camp, north of Berlin. The university was then closed and the news sent shockwaves through Krakow.

The General Government

Foreign ministers Joachim von Ribbentrop and Vyacheslav Molotov had signed a non-aggression pact on behalf of the Third Reich and the Soviet Union on 23 August 1939. At the same time they had agreed a secret protocol to divide Poland in half, and the new border would run along the Vistula, the Pisa, the Narew and the San. On 17 September German troops were moving up to the rivers as the Red Army crossed the Polish border. Five days later Wehrmacht and Soviet soldiers paraded side-by-side in the city of Brest, 125 miles east of Warsaw. Ribbentrop and Molotov signed the 'Treaty of Friendship, Cooperation and Demarcation' on the 28th, agreeing the new border.

Hitler refused to grant Poland occupied territory status so that international conventions could be ignored. He explained why he had done so to Lieutenant General Wilhelm Keitel, Supreme Command of the Wehrmacht, on 17 October: *"Low standards of living must be maintained in that country; we only want to obtain labour from there."*

Nine days later the German occupied area was split in two and while the north was incorporated into the Reich, the rest was going to be ruled by the General Government. Reich Minister and Doctor of Law, Hans Frank, was appointed governor and his first directive was that German was the official language.

A New Capital
On 4 November 1939 Governor-General *Gruppenführer* Hans Frank (soon to be promoted to *Obergruppenführer*) spoke to Hitler about the future of Warsaw and Krakow. Hitler intended to demolish Warsaw castle and leave the city a ruined shell while Krakow became the capital of the General Government. The same day flags decorated the main road into the city, buildings were lit up and officials, police

Governor-General Hans Frank.

and Germans lined the main road into the city as Frank made a triumphant entrance and occupied his new office and home in Royal Castle on Wawel Hill; or as the Germans called it 'The Castle' (*Die Burg*).

German performers put on a huge evening spectacle and after the banquet, Hans Frank ensured *"Everyone complying with the creative work of our Reich will be able to live, work, and develop. We come to this country not as savage conquerors, but as the guarantors of work ordered and managed in the German way."* They were encouraging words but they were far from the truth.

Governor-General Frank presented himself as ruling king rather than a governor as Dr Josef Bühler's civil servants set up a dozen departments, covering all aspects of life, and two offices controlling banking and taxation. Frank and Bühler ruled over 11 million people between them, including 9.8 million Poles, 1.1 million Jews, 375,000 Ukrainians and 61,000 Germans.

The General Government was divided into districts, each run by a chief (they were known as governors after 1942), and they split their areas into urban and rural counties; they were all administered by Germans. The city chief Dr Ernst Zorner convened the first meeting of the Krakow District in the Palace under the Rams (*Palac Pod Baranami*), on the Market Square (*Rynek Glówny*), on 10 November.

The administration's first objective was to purge the country of its leaders and intelligentsia, either through imprisonment, deportation or execution. Another early objective was to exploit the area's economy, resources and labour force. German culture would be imposed on the area, while Polish culture would be suppressed, under a process called Germanization. Ultimately the plan was to *"destroy the Polish people as a nation"* and create *"a new living space for Germans"*. Eventually part of that plan would be the mass murder of Poland's Jews.

A New Administration
SS chief, Heinrich Himmler, had issued a directive on 30 October 1939 which would have a huge impact on the racial make-up of

General Government. All Polish citizens of German descent would be added to the *German Peoples' List* (*Deutsch Völker Liste*) while tens of thousands of Poles and Jews were to be relocated from annexed areas into the General Government area. It was part of the Nazi's master plan for *Living Space* (*Lebensraum*).

Krakow was already overcrowded because Poles and Jews were being moved out of their homes to make way for the 20,000 Germans who would work for the government. The problem was increased when an additional 14,000 Poles and Jews settled in the Krakow area as a result of Himmler's directive.

Polish organizations were also moved out of their offices to make way for German government departments.

Hans Frank moved into the Diocesan Museum apartments, on Wawel Hill while the General Government headquarters occupied the Academy of Mining (now the University of Science and Technology), at 30 Aleja Adama Mickiewicza on the west side of the city. The rest of the government occupied buildings in the adjacent Three Bards area of the city (named after three poets, Juliusz Slowacki, Adam Mickiewicz and Zygmunt Krasinski).

The SS and Police commandant, *SS-Obergruppenführer* Friedrich-Wilhelm Krüger based himself in the castle complex on Wawel Hill while his headquarters were at Legionnaires House at 7 Aleja 3 Maja. The Security Police, Security Service and Gestapo were at Silesian House at 2 Pomorska. Many other organizations had their headquarters in the city; including the local Nazi Party, the German Bank and the German Post Office.

Chapter 3

Ruling Occupied Poland

While the Einsatzkommandos reigned terror on the streets, the General Government set about introducing the decrees which would rule Polish life for over four years. They would affect all aspects of life and divide the people into three, each with different rules; the Germans, the Poles and the Jews.

Establishing the Regime

The General Government always deliberated before introducing a new decree because they wanted to be sure it could be enforced, maintaining a respect for the law. While they stopped Poles from entering many bars and restaurants, it allocated Polish-only establishments to stop 'needless resentment' which would make them 'feel treated on equal terms with Jews'.

The authorities knew Polish nationalists and intellectuals liked to meet in cafés and restaurants to discuss their ideas. They could send agents to monitor public places whereas they could not control private meetings if they closed everywhere down.

The city's best restaurants were made German-only as were certain cinemas and theatres. The Wehrmacht, the police and the SS were also allocated their own establishments but soldiers often tried to get into other venues because they had better entertainment. Prostitutes were banned from German venues and they could not work the streets in the German quarter. The Health Office dealt with the need by setting up German-only brothels in buildings which had served the Jewish community.

Poles were turned into second class citizens as the number of apartheid style laws increased. Trams were split into German and Polish sections and Poles were banned from certain public spaces and even from sitting on park benches.

Redesigning the City

Germany invaded the Netherlands, Belgium and France on 10 May 1940 and all three had surrendered by 22 June. Although Nazi Germany considered invading Great Britain, the failure to achieve air supremacy in the Battle of Britain resulted in a change of plan; it would attack the Soviet Union instead. The change triggered Operation Otto, the plan to turn the General Government into a huge manufacturing base and source of forced labour for the Third Reich. A deportation camp was set up in the south-east suburbs of Krakow where forced labourers would be quarantined before deportation.

Starting on 8 July the title 'occupied Polish territories' was replaced by 'General Government'. People could no longer refer to themselves as Poles; they were members of 'the population of the General Government'.

Operation Otto also prompted the General Government to divide Krakow into three residential quarters: German, Polish and Jewish. Plans for a German-only residential area around the government district on the west side of the city were discussed for the first time on 6 September 1940. It would stretch from the Gestapo headquarters in the north, through the former Polish Mining Academy and Blonia Park, to Wawel Castle.

Frank's plan was to turn Krakow into the 'Nuremberg of the East', a copy of the 'most German of German cities' and he had big ideas for the government district. Architect Hubert Ritter had been invited to turn them into working plans but they argued and he had to leave. The design project was then given to the city Building Department and its staff followed the Governor-General's instructions. The boundaries were decided in February 1941 and a month later an order was issued to take the first step, the formation of the Jewish ghetto in the Podgórze district on the south bank of the Vistula.

On 16 April 1941 Hans Frank had the neighbouring rural

Wawel Castle overlooks the River Vistula.

communities incorporated into Krakow, more than tripling the area and bringing 321,000 people under the control of the new city governor, *Stadthauptmann* Carl Schmidt. A huge social gathering was held to celebrate the creation of the super city in the City Council offices in Wielopolskich Palace on 13 June. With the city divided, the next city governor, *Stadthauptmann* Rudolf Pavlu, announced that no more Poles or Jews would be allowed to move into Krakow after 22 September.

The Building Department immediately went to work as loans were granted to improve and convert buildings while new structures were approved. Rooms in the Royal Castle on Wawel Hill were renovated in a German style and the Kings' Stables were replaced by an office building. Houses were demolished around the perimeter of the castle and an area was cleared at the south-east corner for a new access road.

There were plans to convert the façades of the buildings surrounding the Market Square to give the area a German appearance. The City Council offices would also be upgraded as would the accommodation for government officials along what would become Reichsstrasse (now Krolewska), on the north-west side of the city.

Germanizing Krakow

Plans were put in place to remove Polish symbolism from the streets and the first monument was removed from Matejki Square on 11 December 1939; it commemorated the 1410 Polish victory over the Teutonic Knights in the battle of Grunwald (Tannenberg). On 11 January 1940 Tadeusz Kosciuszko's monument was removed from Wawel Hill. Kosciuszko was commander of the Polish National Armed Forces during the 1794 uprising against Russia and Prussia. In August two statues of nineteenth century poets, Adam Mickiewicz and Aleksander Fredro, were removed from the Market Square.

The first anniversary celebration in the Market Square.

The Market Square was renamed Adolf Hitler Platz on 1 September, anniversary of the German invasion; the main streets were given names such as Reich Street, Wehrmacht Street and Movement Street (referring to the Nazi Party movement). All other streets would eventually have their Polish names translated into German. The name of the capital was Germanized to Krakau on 15 August 1941 and the eagle on the city's coat of arms was replaced with the swastika a month later.

Steps were also taken to Germanize cultural and scientific institutions. The Institute for German East Labour was established in the Jagiellonian University library in April 1940 and it had two objectives. The first was to research the natural resources in the Krakow area, ready for exploitation. The second was to hold exhibitions and publish magazines supporting the Germanization projects.

Frank also appointed a Reich Commissioner to introduce German customs and culture, helping to turn the General Government into a satellite country of the Third Reich. The Propaganda and Public Enlightenment Department also spread the word through the radio, posters and newspapers like the *Krakow Journal* (*Krakauer Zeitung*).

Making Way for the Germans
Thousands of German officials moved to Krakow to run the capital of the General Government (the number of Germans would rise to one-in-five). To begin with the food situation was better in Krakow than across the rest of the Reich but the situation deteriorated when the tide of the war turned and rationing was increased. There were black market opportunities but the Poles had more opportunities for bartering with their families and friends.

The Germans often complained that the Polish shop owners were favouring their friends. They also moaned they did not have time to queue for provisions outside their working hours. The authorities responded by forcing shops to open longer and have German-only hours in the mornings and evenings. Germans were also forbidden from listening to foreign radio stations and subject to the night time curfew, because members of the underground and criminals were roaming the streets.

Hitler Youth parade through the city.

The influx of Germans created huge housing problems. The Building Police (*Baupolizei*) counted nearly 40,000 apartments across the city but half only had one room, three out of four had a shared bathroom and few were gas-heated. The survey concluded that only twenty dwellings were classified suitable for German occupation. Although the highest ranking officials enjoyed extravagant lifestyles in the best apartments, the hundreds of low level officials lived in small apartments with basic furnishings and few amenities. The Housing Office (*Wohnungsamt*) allotted two rooms to senior officials and a single room to junior administrators until improved housing could be built. To begin with Germans were housed in unoccupied apartments where the owner could not be traced; also Poles and Jews were forced to let out rooms to officials.

In the first quarter of 1941 60,000 Jews were forced to leave their properties and either move in with friends and relatives or into the ghetto, on the south bank of the River Vistula. Around 8,000 apartments were emptied and Poles were moved into them, so Germans could occupy the best ones.

The Housing Office also rented out empty apartments and businesses, some left by people who had moved to the countryside and some confiscated from Jews. All Jews without a permit were forcibly moved out of Krakow starting at the end of 1940 and each person was only allowed to take 25kg of luggage, leaving their furniture behind.

All furniture and household items abandoned by the Jews and Poles became state property because nothing was to be wasted. The Furniture Management Office compiled inventories for the Trusteeship Office, on behalf of the Office for Economic Matters. Anything worth less than its transport cost was sold to the new Polish occupants; everything else was taken to a warehouse ready for resale or distribution to the arriving Germans.

German officials were constantly reminded to be frugal by the regime but many acquired extra comforts through stealing, bribery and extortion. After February 1942 German officials had to itemize everything they had been given as well, and list illegally acquired items; checks were made to see they were telling the truth.

The Railways and Postal Service

On 31 October 1939 the *German Post East* (*Deutsche Post Osten*) opened its headquarters in Krakow and took over Polish Postal, Telegraph and Telephone Services. Its staff were responsible for delivering, monitoring and censoring mail and calls.

The Polish State Railways' engines and rolling stock were confiscated at the end of September when Poland's railway system was incorporated into the German State Railways. The *General Directorate of the Railways in the East* was established in Krakow to control military transports in the General Government.

In October 1940 plans to improve the rail network were put into action under Operation Otto and 30,000 German and Polish railwaymen prepared for the invasion of the Soviet Union over the next nine months. A new railway line was built around the north side of the city and an autobahn was built to the south. The Central railway station was also enlarged and modernized. The number of trains the Directorate could handle increased from 80 trains a day to 220;

improvements under Codename *Ostbahn* would increase the number further.

Krakow's railway station (*Hauptbahnhof Krakau*) was a bottleneck on the lines running west to east, so the Directorate built a new line bypassing the city and extended the railway station. It meant trains could carry troops and ammunition quickly to the front while the hospital trains brought casualties to the city's clinics.

Stealing and Corruption

SS-Gruppenführer Reinhard Heydrich's *Reich Security Main Office* (*Reichssicherheitshauptamt*, RHSA) delegated the Trusteeship Main Office East to search libraries and art galleries. Eleven days later Frank issued a decree to remove *'all kinds of valuable public property'*. The inspectors went to work plundering the city's private, public and religious art collections.

The former Austrian art commissioner, Kajetan Muhlmann, eventually catalogued 500 of the most valuable and most German items. The best were sent to the Reich where they ended up in the hands of top Nazis, including Adolf Hitler's private collection in Linz museum. Dr Hans Posse assessed many Polish works as poor quality while priceless Jewish items were destroyed or melted down; any art pieces and paintings deemed to be corrupt or immoral were also destroyed.

To begin with Frank did not object to treasures leaving the General Government but soon ignored Himmler's directive and collected everything in Krakow when he realized there was money to be made. He used a few items to decorate Wawel Castle, while others ended up in his offices and his houses and some were rented out to senior Nazis. The result was many items went missing in transit while others were kept hidden in Wawel Castle in poor conditions. (Ironically ninety per cent of Polish works of art were saved at the end of the war because Frank had kept them in Krakow.)

While Frank had a large residence in Bavaria and his apartments in Krakow, he also restored Potocki Palace in Krzeszowice village, north-west of Krakow. He renamed it Haus Kressendorf and used it as his summer residence. The Governor of Krakow used Przegorzaly Castle, west of the city as his out-of-town home.

With so much money and property about, there were opportunities for corruption and it went right to the top. The Governor of the Galician District, Dr Karl Lasch, accused the Governor-General's office of misconduct after he was arrested for embezzling funds in January 1942. The deputy head of administration in Hans Frank's Office was questioned and he in turn denounced his superior.

The judge reported the matter to *SS-Reichsführer* Heinrich Himmler and Head of the Nazi Party's Chancellery Martin Bormann. The Governor was accused of maintaining a lavish lifestyle by buying luxury items from Jews for a fraction of their price, while his wife Magdalena was indicted for amassing a huge collection of fur coats; his sister was also named.

The Head of the Reich Chancellery, Dr Hans Lammers, summoned Frank to Hitler's headquarters to meet Bormann and Himmler in March 1942. He countered that his lifestyle was a *"necessity of grand-style representation in front of the hostile population, since only truly lordly characters can reign in the East"*. He denied all knowledge of his wife's activities and condemned her actions; he also said he was on bad terms with his sister and knew nothing about her dealings.

While the case against Frank was dropped, he did not forget the trouble caused by his long-time friend. Lasch was accused of corruption, making false transactions and currency violations. He was sent to Auschwitz and was either shot on Himmler's instructions or committed suicide.

Chapter 4

The First Year Under the Nazis

On 15 September 1939 the *Führer* had told Hans Frank that the General Government area was to be *"exploited mercilessly and turned into rubble in economic, social, cultural and political terms"*. On 31 October Frank made the following statement: *"Poles must be enabled to be educated only to the extent that would make them realize that they have no prospects whatsoever as a nation?"* The Krakovians were about to find out what he meant.

Stamping Out Education
Around 120 people were arrested and held hostage to stop anyone celebrating Polish Independence Day on 11 November; and stop anyone carrying out sabotage. Celebratory posters were banned and an order threatened to execute one member of any household displaying one.

Once the day had passed hundreds of secondary school teachers were arrested and sent to concentration camps under 'Krakow's Second Special Action'. Polish secondary schools were taken over by the army and police while students were crammed into vocational colleges to learn a manual trade. Primary schools were allowed to stay open but cultural subjects, including geography, history and literature were banned; physical education was also taken off the curriculum.

A month later Polish history and geography text books were removed from shops so students could not educate themselves.

Meanwhile, the Nazi printing presses worked around the clock to produce magazines filled with trivial articles and propaganda. Subscription was obligatory but few read them.

The Secret Teachers' Organization was organized to run private classes. Some lecturers and teachers gave secret history and culture lessons with stolen books but they faced imprisonment in a concentration camp if they were caught while their students would be deported. The Government Delegation for Poland, the Government in Exile's agency in Poland, would form an Education and Culture Department in January 1941 and Krakow's Regional School Office would try and provide support for the teachers.

Once the Polish education system had been dealt with, all Jewish schools were closed down on 11 December 1939. Jewish students were expelled from Polish schools and Jewish teachers were sacked. The schools opened their doors for one day only so the teachers' and children's names could be added to the census.

The Special Service (*Sicherheitsdienst*) spent the winter months compiling lists of lawyers, doctors, teachers, social activists, artists, priests and other religious leaders. Starting on 30 March 1940, 35,000 men and women were arrested across Poland in just twelve weeks in what the General Government called the Extraordinary Pacification Action (*Ausserordentliche Befriedungsaktion*, or AB Action).

Working in the City

On 26 October 1939 decrees concerning work were announced. Poles had to work for the minimum wage, the working day was extended to ten hours and annual leave was reduced to six days. Everybody had to carry two forms of identification, their personal ID card (*Kennkarte*) and their work card (*Arbeitskarte*). They also needed an access pass if they had to leave their own district when they walked to work.

The Labour Office managed all job opportunities, authorized job changes and gave the unemployed work. The office also organized the deportation of Polish workers to Germany. They were encouraged to work in the Reich with a promise of more money and a better life; they did not get either. Workers were gathered in a transit camp on

A Polish policeman checks a Jew's papers.

Waska and then made the train journey west. They had to work hard for poor wages and had to wear the letter 'P' on their clothes, marking them out as Polish immigrants. They were again subject to curfews and prohibited from mixing with Germans or visiting public places.

People soon stopped volunteering and workers were summoned or rounded up and transported to Germany against their will. Some paid bribes or faked sickness to avoid leaving home. Others made a living out of going in somebody's place, only to escape en route.

In March 1941 the Building Service introduced compulsory service of three months, and longer for young men. They were housed in poor conditions and were given the hardest jobs, including construction, drainage and renovation work. The Building Service closed in July 1944 as the push to send workers to Germany was stepped up.

Rationing

Food was always short in Krakow and many items were rationed, including milk, flour, eggs, noodles, kasha (porridge style cereal), sugar and fruit preserves (jam and honey). Soap, candles, paraffin, shoes and textiles were also rationed. But the availability of items changed every week and women spent long hours queuing as they tried to feed and clothe their families. Hans Frank made it clear where his priorities lay in feeding the population in a speech on 23 April 1940: *"I am not interested in the Jews at all. The last thing I care about is whether or not they have anything to eat. The Poles fall into another category, as long as I may need them. I will feed these Poles in a way that the remains at our disposal will be distributed."*

Coupons were issued according to nationality with the Germans first, then Ukrainians, then Poles and finally Jews; those with demanding jobs were given extra. Coupons were distributed by apartment block caretakers or house managers and not everyone got their fair share. Some people headed into the country to barter with family or peasants but this option disappeared on 21 January 1940. Peasants were ordered to hand over all spare milk, fats, grains, fodder and cattle for the German army or for distribution across the Reich. Meat was particularly difficult to obtain because small butchers were closed down and all meat came from the municipal abattoirs. Some people secretly bred animals to produce dairy products or to slaughter but they faced imprisonment if they were caught.

The shortage of food resulted in a thriving black market and a few entrepreneurs specialized in smuggling or stealing items to sell or barter. While a few smugglers and profiteers became rich, informers and blackmailers became wealthy reporting them to the authorities. Anyone caught was deported to a concentration camp or Germany.

Street trading had always been a big part of Krakow's city life and thousands attended open air markets across the city. Market squares were regularly searched and roundups were often made; several hundred people were seized on 20 November 1942 alone and they were deported to the Reich. A huge street market called the Tandem was closed on 8 December 1942 but people continued to trade, despite regular police raids.

Several organizations did what they could to send aid to the Poles and Jews in Poland. Count Adam Ronikier's Central Welfare Council (RGO) had been established with German approval in Warsaw in November 1939 and it operated through the Polish Welfare Committee. It distributed aid sent from the USA under American supervision.

In April 1940 the General Government established the Head Welfare Council (NRO) to coordinate the activities of the Central Welfare Council, the Ukrainian Central Council and the Jewish Social Self-Help association. It collected medicines, clothes and foodstuffs sent by the Commission for Polish Relief (CPR, also known as the Hoover Committee), the International Red Cross and the General Government. The organizations worked hard to help prisoners, refugees and displaced persons; they also distributed aid to the elderly, to the disabled and for children. Krakow's children suffered particularly badly and Roza Lubienska set up the Committee for Helping Children and Youth in November 1940. Her team distributed extra meals and organized summer camps until the German authorities banned them.

The Polish Government in Exile forwarded donations to the

German Red Cross while the American Jewish Joint Distribution Committee (known as the Joint) sent money. But American aid stopped when Germany declared war on the USA in December 1941 and the Council began organizing charity collections to make up the difference. Archbishop Adam Sapieha also asked the people of Krakow to make donations and monthly collections were held in churches across the city.

Newspapers and Radios

On 31 October 1939 Dr Joseph Goebbels, Reich Minister for Propaganda and Public Enlightenment, announced *"the entire Polish information system must be liquidated. The Poles should not own radio receivers; they must only be left with newspapers, while an opinion-forming press must never be allowed."* The authorities started by closing down all Polish and Jewish newspapers.

They were replaced by German newspapers and the underground called for a boycott on what they called the 'Reptile Press'. The *Krakow Messenger* was filled with propaganda and the Nazis' view of the world news; it was nicknamed *Under the Tail* because it was only useful for wiping your backside. The appearance of a spoof copy, mocking and parodying the authorities, caused a huge stir across the city.

The authorities ordered everyone to hand their radio receivers and aerials in on 11 January 1940. Loudspeakers were installed on many streets and they reported official notices, announcements about the war, lists of people sentenced to death and the occasional sombre tune. Their constant drone led to them being called 'yappers'.

Cinemas, Theatres and Concerts

The Krakow branch of the Ministry for Propaganda and Enlightenment censored all Polish material and removed Jewish references from the arts. Theatres, cinema and other light entertainment venues were split into German and Polish-only venues while Jews were banned from using them.

The General Government started producing a weekly newsreel in May 1940 and it opened all cinema performances. Pre-war Polish

The reopening of the National Theatre of the General Government.

films were heavily censored so that only those with pro-German or bland story lines were screened. Propaganda documentaries were also shown and the first one covered the Wehrmacht's invasion of Poland, with a twisted story line which blamed Great Britain and Prime Minister Neville Chamberlain for the rapid collapse of the Polish armed forces.

On 31 October 1939 Dr Joseph Goebbels announced that Poles would be banned from theatres and the Polish Theatre Company closed down two weeks later. German producers and actors were hired while Polish backstage personnel were put to work, sometimes under the threat of deportation. On 1 September 1940 the 'Juliusz Slowacki Theatre' reopened under a new name, the 'National Theatre of the General Government'. But German plays were nothing but boring propaganda stories and one performance called 'Quarantine' was the story of recent anti-typhus work; it had won the Propaganda Ministry's competition. Poles rarely attended the biased plays and tear gas was thrown in the auditorium during the final performance.

Dr Hans Rohr arrived from Munich in the spring of 1940 to organize a Krakow symphony orchestra and musicians had to register with the Propaganda Department. The first concert was held in front of Hans Frank in June 1940 in the yard of the Collegium Mains, in the Jagiellonian University. The college was the oldest building in the university and it had been turned into the Institute for Eastern Workers, an office which supervised Germanization projects. A second philharmonic orchestra was formed in the late summer and it held its first concert on 14 October 1940.

Rohr died in December 1940 and although Hitler posthumously decorated him, there were rumours he had been poisoned because he was too friendly towards the Poles. Later conductors were Rudolf Hindemith and Hans Swarowsky. Their musicians and choristers had extra ration coupons and special ID cards, which stopped them being deported.

Anniversary Celebrations

On 1 September 1940, the first anniversary of the invasion, the General Government pulled out all the stops to remind the Polish that the Germans were in charge. Krakow's buildings were festooned with swastika flags and there were celebrations in the Market Square as the Germans renamed it Adolf Hitler Square. Governor-General Frank opened an art exhibition called 'German Activity along the Vistula' in the Palace of Arts (*Palac Sztuki*). But while the Germans turned out in force to celebrate, the Poles preferred to stay at home.

Chapter 5

Organizing Terror on
the Streets

A proclamation on 26 October 1939 made it clear how the Germans intended to govern the General Government:

> *"Under a just rule everyone will earn his bread by work. On the other hand, there will be no room for political agitators, shady dealers, and Jewish exploiters in a territory that is under German sovereignty. Any attempt at recalcitrance against the decrees issued and against peace and order in the Polish territories will be crushed with the strong weapons of the Greater German Reich and with the most ruthless severity. But those who comply with the just orders of our Reich, which will be in absolute accord with your mode of life, shall be allowed to work in safety."*

Now we must look at the organizations which questioned, arrested and executed those who failed to comply with the draconian laws.

The Security Police and Security Service Take Over
Once the initial wave of arrests had been made, it was time for new organizations to take over security from the Einsatzgruppen in the streets of Krakow. The Security Service (*Sicherheitsdienst, SD*) and the Secret State Police (*Geheime Staatspolizei, Gestapo*) detected enemies of the state, using agents and informants. The SD targeted

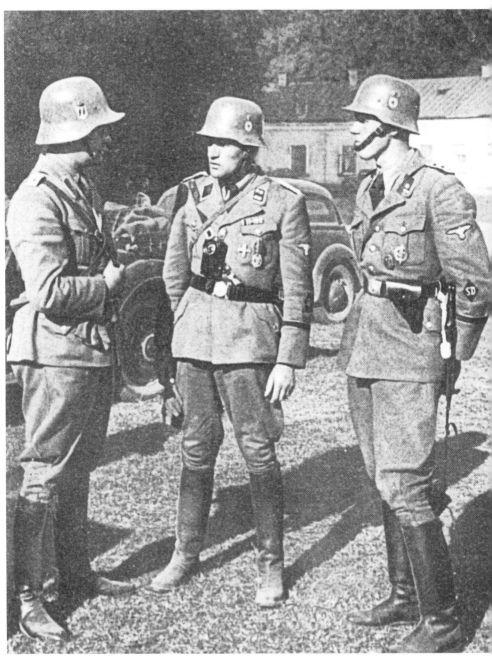

Members of the Security Service SD get their orders from the SS.

the intelligentsia, groups and associations as well as political, nationalist and religious activists, including the Jews. The Gestapo dealt with communists, attacks on the economy, the press and persons accused of committing treason. Their areas of interest often clashed. The Security Police (*Sicherheitspolizei* or *SiPo*) were responsible for arresting the accused and for conducting round-ups and searches in conjunction with the SD's and Gestapo's activities. Between them they would maintain terror on the streets of Krakow.

On 31 October 1939, Hans Frank issued a decree *"on preventing incidents of violence against the German Reich or the supreme German authorities in the General Government"*. It introduced the death penalty for *"acts committed to the detriment of the Reich, the officials, the German citizens in the GG and the property of the GG"*. The Security Police summary courts would administer the trials and pass sentence. The following day Streckenbach, commander of the *Einsatzkommandos*, was promoted to head of the Security Police and Security Service (*Sipo* and *Sicherheitsdienst*) of all occupied Polish territory. (He would be followed by *SS-Oberführer* Karl Eberhard Schöngarth in January 1941 and *SS-Oberführer* Walther Bierkamp in July 1943.)

Streckenbach reported to *SS-Obergruppenführer* Friedrich-Wilhelm Krüger, the Higher SS and Police commandant in the General Government. Krüger would be dismissed on 9 November 1943 for quarrelling with Hans Frank and replaced by *SS-Obergruppenführer* Wilhelm Koppe. Both men were second only to Governor-General Frank, and they had virtually unrestricted power across the General Government.

Over 20,000 Polish people would be murdered by the time the *Einsatzkommandos* disbanded. *Einsatzgruppen I* had gained a fearful reputation across Silesia by the time it disbanded and its members converted into regular police officers on 20 November. *Einsatzkommando* 2/1 became the *Krakow District Security Police and Security Service Command* (KdS) and its orders were to *"liquidate enemies of the new order, combat resistance and pro-independence organizations, supervise extermination of the Jewish people and prevent the sabotage of production and trade."* It was still based at Silesian House at 2 Pomorska St and its Section IV was better known as the Gestapo.

Some of the commandants were:

SS-Obersturmbannführer Bruno Müller (November and December 1939)

SS-Sturmbannführer Walter Huppenkothen (December 1939 to January 1940)

SS-Standartenführer Ludwig Hahn (January 1940 to August 1940)

SS-Obersturmbannführer Max Grosskopf (August 1940 to Summer 1943)

SS-Sturmbannführer Rudolf Batz (1943)

The Gestapo

The Gestapo thrived on people reporting on others and its officers spent a great deal of time completing and correlating denunciations in their search for suspicious activity. People visited or wrote to the Gestapo for a range of reasons; some were looking for a financial reward or personal gain, some were being blackmailed and some did it because they had a grudge, a dispute or a vendetta against the accused. Agents working at the main post office intercepted and destroyed many letters addressed to the Gestapo offices.

Once a suspect had been identified, they were invited to attend Silesian House at 2 Pomorska for questioning. It was made clear they would be considered guilty and arrested if they did not. An interview began routinely, involving questions relating to the denunciation and the typing up of the answers. The lucky few were allowed to leave with a warning but many faced the next stage.

The rest had their hands cuffed behind their back and were taken to another room where two interrogators and an interpreter were waiting. They suggested the prisoner would be released if they told the truth and the array of weapons on the table make it clear what would happen if they did not. Then the questioning began, reinforced with random acts of violence.

Prisoners were caned, whipped and beaten with clubs;

Silesian House, the Gestapo Headquarters.

sometimes they were suffocated with a gasmask. Other interrogators preferred to twist a prisoner's arms behind their back and suspend them from a hook on the wall or door frame. Repetitive exercises, such as holding items with arms outstretched or knee bends were also used to vary the physical and mental pains inflicted.

The tortures continued until the prisoner passed out and they were then revived with cold water or burning cigarettes. Questioning was carried out at all hours to keep the prisoners fatigued and they were only returned to their cells when the interrogators were tired. The beatings could go on for days and only ended when the prisoner broke or the Gestapo officers felt they had no more to tell; some died under questioning. The survivors were often shot soon afterwards.

The Gestapo used informers to catch people breaking the law or working for the underground. Informers were motivated by a range of things, including fear, greed and envy. Some reported crimes in return for money while others were blackmailed. Occasionally people broke under torture and ended up working for the Gestapo in return for their release. The underground viewed informants as traitors and publicized their names and addresses in their press.

The Polish Police

The General Government had reorganized the Polish Police and made it subordinate to the uniformed German police force, the Order Police (*Ordnungspolizei* or *Orpo*). Polish officers were not allowed to resign and they had to work as auxiliaries to the German forces. They were known as 'navy-blues' due to the colour of their uniforms.

While they carried out normal police duties, such as directing traffic and collecting fines, they also had to take part in round-ups and arrests. The navy-blues were seen as traitors who worked for the Germans but some were involved in underground activities. They would interfere with the police actions and try to help people avoid arrest or deportation. The Polish Police chief, Major Franciszek Erhard, was arrested and executed early in 1944 for his work in the underground movement. He had saved the lives of hundreds of Poles and Jews during his five years of service.

The Prisons

The Security Police used the police prison at 7 Montelupich and the court prison at 3 Senacka, known as St Michael's prison; it had auxiliary prisons at 3 Czarneckiego and 2 Wielicka. They also used the Security Police cells at 2 Pomorska.

All detainees were eventually moved to 7 Montelupich, Krakow's prison since 1918, known locally as the Monte or the Montelupa. The prison was taken over by the Office of the Chief of the Security Police and the Security Service in November 1939 and on 23 December, 100 criminals were moved out and put to work building a labour camp, to free up cells for new prisoners. The Gestapo took over the facility in March 1941 and the adjacent workhouse was turned into a women's prison at the end of the year.

People ended up in custody for different reasons. Many were arrested because their name was on a list, either because of their work, their politics or their religious beliefs. Others were held because they had been involved in, or were suspected of being involved in, anti-government crimes, ranging from sabotage and murder to stealing and black market activities. Some were arrested because they had been denounced by neighbours or associates. Many were held only because they had been in the wrong place at the wrong time.

Prisoners were held in a small cell furnished only with a stool, a table and a jail bed but no blanket. They only had a jug for water, a tin for holding food, a spoon to eat with and a bucket to use as a toilet. While they could wash with the water they had no soap or towel.

Executions

Prisoners were led out to dig their own graves the day before their execution and then they spent a long night in the death cell, praying, singing hymns, writing letters and confessing their sins. The following morning they were gagged with plaster of Paris and led out into the prison yard to be shot.

After November 1939 most condemned prisoners were handed over to the Heaven Kommando (*Himmelkommando*). They were loaded onto trucks early in the morning and driven out of the city. Once at their destination, they were dragged off the vehicles and frog-marched to the execution site. Locals were then forced to bury the bodies. The Heaven Kommando shot many of the professionals, including lawyers, doctors and teachers, who were rounded up in the Extraordinary Pacification Action in the spring of 1940. Around 440 prisoners (including 18 women) would be shot in an old fort near Krzeslawice, seven miles north-east of the city, while another 2,000 were executed in a clay quarry in the Przegorzaly Woods, four miles west of the city.

Certain categories of prisoners were deported to concentration camps to be executed and the first group was put on a train on 20 June 1940 and sent the short distance to Auschwitz; they were some of the first inmates in the new camp. Other transports went to Gross-Rosen concentration camp, west of Wroclaw, and Sachsenhausen concentration camp, north of Berlin; women were taken to Ravensbrück camp, also north of Berlin.

Mass executions were held in hidden locations outside the city.

The authorities ordered all officers, retired officers and reserve officers of the Polish Army to register or face the death penalty in the summer of 1941. The regular and retired officers were arrested over the winter while 2,000 reserve officers were rounded up between 16 and 23 April 1942. They were deported to Auschwitz, where most of them were murdered. Around the same time, the Gestapo arrested all the painters, sculptors and actors who frequented the 'Plastic Café' at 3 Lobzowska. They were sent to Auschwitz and executed by firing squad on 27 May 1942.

In June 1942 the authorities closed the mental institution in Kobierzyn, south-west of Krakow. Around 500 patients were put into cattle trucks, taken to Birkenau and gassed while thirty bedridden patients were murdered; twenty-five Jews who buried the bodies were also killed. The hospital was then turned over to the SS and the Hitler Youth.

The city's defence deputy, *Oberst* Wolfgang Wieser, had suggested carrying out public executions to stop people supporting acts of sabotage back on the 24 April 1941. Over a year later, Hans

Frank took up his suggestion when a train was derailed near Plaszow railway station. A public gallows was built near the site of the crime and seven people were executed on 26 June 1942. Their bodies were left hanging for several days to increase the impact of the warning. A few days later there was an attempt on the life of a Polish policeman in the Wola Duchacka district, on the south side of the city, and eleven locals were hung on makeshift gallows.

To begin with the authorities would announce the names and addresses of hostages being held in prison and those who had been sentenced to death. After November 1943 'death notices' were printed and posted on bill boards around the city as a more permanent reminder.

On 2 October 1943 the decree controlling the summary courts was altered so it covered many more violations. The courts could also pass the death sentence on hostages and even innocent people loosely associated with a crime as a deterrent. The first mass execution of twenty prisoners took place on 20 October 1943, after a clerk employed at the Labour Office on Mazowiecka was killed. Another group were shot the following day on Wasowicza (now Smolensk Street).

A week later a group of men with their hands tied behind their back were led into Bawol Square, in the Kazimierz district. They were ordered to spread out and were gunned down. The guards finished off the injured and then made passers-by throw the corpses onto a waiting lorry so they could be taken away. These were just the first three of over 100 mass executions carried out on the streets of Krakow over the next fifteen months.

Round-ups

The first round-up began on the night of 6 December 1939 when auxiliaries surrounded the Jewish district of Kazimierz. Everyone was confined to their apartments for three days while the police searched them, smashing and stealing their property. Many were beaten and others were arrested. It was just the first of what would be an almost daily occurrence of round-ups and property searches across Krakow.

A round-up begins.

The police randomly cordoned off a street or square, lined everyone up, searched them and checked their papers. They also targeted public places, including the flea market and the railway station as well as restaurants, cafés and cinemas. Even factories and offices were searched and the police rifled through desks, cabinets and briefcases, in the hunt for incriminating evidence. Polish national holidays such as Constitution Day (3 May) and Independence Day (11 November) were popular days to carry out raids because there were many people on the streets.

In the early hours of 29 July 1943, during a search of the Wola Justowska district, west of the city centre, the German police discovered three print shops, and the Gestapo moved in to arrest people named on pre-prepared lists. Suspects were questioned, sentenced and the guilty had a cross chalked on the back of their jacket. They were led into a field, made to lie face down and shot.

Kazimierz district, where Poles had replaced the Jews, was raided again on 22 September 1943. Police units surrounded the area and called everyone onto the streets. Each house was searched and marked with a letter D, to denote it was clear. Everyone but the elderly and the children were marched to a school on Waska and had their documents checked. Some were imprisoned while others would be sent to work in Germany.

The largest round-up in Krakow was made on Sunday, 6 August 1944. The General Government had been shocked by the Warsaw uprising and they were worried there could be similar disturbances across Krakow. Around 6,000 people were dragged from their homes or off the streets and most were taken to Plaszow's concentration camp. The raids paralyzed the city and many factories and companies had to close until their employees had been released. Many never returned; they were deported to Germany.

Deportations

During the course of the war over 1.2 million Poles moved through Krakow en route to work in the Third Reich. They were held in transit camps around the city and then taken to the railway station and deported in cattle trucks to labour camps.

A recruitment campaign was held in February 1940, supported by fictitious letters from Poles enjoying the work. Hans Frank made an unsuccessful appeal for extra workers four months later and round-ups were held to get enough workers.

A forced labour camp was set up in the Wola Duchacka district, just south of the Plaszow camp, in 1942 and a separate Polish section was set up in the Jewish labour camp the following year. In January 1944 all the forced labour camps were merged to form one concentration camp as labour levies were introduced. Thousands of summonses were sent out by the Labour Office, instructing people to report to a transit camp but many avoided deportation through bribery, false sick notes or forged letters stating they had protected jobs. Others escaped from the trains en route to Germany and returned home.

Chapter 6

The Polish Underground

The Nazis did not have it all their own way. Many Poles, some ex-military, some civilians and some Jewish, did what they could to undermine the regime's reign of terror in any way they could. This is the story of resistance in the General Government, but in particular in Krakow.

A State in Exile

Commander-in-Chief Marshal Edward Rydz-Smigly had made plans how to resist the occupation before leaving Poland and the Polish authorities wanted to carry on the war from abroad. Unfortunately, President Ignacy Moscicki and his government were interned in Romania while Rydz-Smigly headed for Hungary.

President Moscicki ended up in exile in Switzerland and he appointed Wladyslaw Raczkiewicz President of the Polish Government in Exile with General Wladyslaw Sikorski as prime minister; Sikorski was also appointed the commander-in-chief. A Polish National Council was appointed instead of electing a parliament and it was recognized by all countries except Nazi Germany and the Soviet Union.

Two Polish Delegations were formed in December 1940 and while one ran the area annexed by Germany the other ran the General Government. The first delegate for the General Government area was Cyryl Ratajski (codename Mountain, Wartski and Heather). The two delegations merged in 1942 and the head of the Delegation was appointed deputy prime minister in April 1944.

There were six deputies, one for each region, and Jan Jakobiec (codename Carpathian and Blackbird) was Krakow's delegate from August 1941 to March 1945. The city was codenamed Mound, Salt and Wisla at different times and it was split into fourteen districts.

The Directorate of Civil Resistance was set up in autumn 1940 to encourage civilians to participate in anti-German activity. It was headed by Tadeusz Seweryn (codenamed Biaiowas, Ignac, and Plough). In August 1943 the Government Delegation issued '*The Pole's Code, a Code of Civic Morals and Imperatives*'. It called for every citizen to obey the Polish Underground State and boycott decrees beneficial to the Germans or detrimental to the Poles. The Code also prohibited Poles from socializing with Germans and instructed them to reduce their professional contacts to a minimum.

The Underground Forms

Underground activity began soon after German troops entered Krakow when Major Kazimierz Kierzkowski (nicknamed the President) established the *White Eagle Organization* (OOB). Polish Army officers made their way to 1 Grottgera, in Krakow's northern suburbs and took the oath: *"I swear before almighty and ubiquitous God that I shall fight with all my strength and abilities to recover a free and independent Poland. I shall keep the organization's secrets."*

Members worked on distributing propaganda to begin with but some turned to organizing self-help and self-defence

General Karaszewicz-Tokarzewski.

groups. Others formed secretive three-man units, called *Trojki*, and they tried to acquire weapons and plan attacks.

The Polish Underground State was formed in Warsaw on 27 September 1939 and the *Polish Victory Service* (SZP) was its resistance movement. General Michal Karaszewicz-Tokarzewski (nicknamed Torwid) arrived in Krakow on 16 October as its commander-in-chief. Officers gathered soldiers together all across

Poland and formed them into over 150 underground groups during the winter of 1939-1940. Those who acknowledged the exiled government in London were authorized and financed.

In October 1939 Colonel Tadeusz Komorowski, Colonel Edward Godlewski and Lieutenant Colonel Klemens Rudnicki formed *Kaerge* (KRG). Unfortunately, the initials came from their surnames, a poor choice of name, and the group had to be disbanded. Other groups were the *Secret Army of Poland* (ZWZ), the *Union for Armed Action* (TAP), the *National Defence Guard* (ZCZ), the *Polish Armed Organization* (GON) and the *Scouting and Guiding Association* (ZHP). Political organizations, like the *Socialist Party's People's Guard*, also formed their own underground groups.

The new Polish Government in exile mistrusted General Karaszewicz-Tokarzewski's Polish Victory Service, believing it would help the pre-war political movement called *Sanitation* (*Sanacja*) take over the country. They need not have worried because the Germans rounded up many of the organization's leaders while the rest fled to Romania.

Sikorski formed the *Union for Armed Struggle* (*Zwiazek Walki Zbrojnej*, ZWZ), on 13 November 1939. This apolitical underground organization promoted resistance activities, carried out sabotage, discouraged collaboration and monitored the political and military situation. It also trained soldiers and gathered weapons so they could go on the offensive when the Red Army reached Poland. The Victory Service put itself under the Union's control, but Lieutenant-General Kazimierz Sosnkowski struggled to keep in touch with his contacts in Poland from his base in France.

Krakow was the Union's Area 4 and the first commander was Colonel Tadeusz Komorowski (codename Korczak). Colonel Julian Filipowicz (codename Horn) helped him organize the city into thirty-two districts and they recruited nearly 14,000 active men and 40,000 reserve men in the first twelve months. But while Komorowski was able to get the volunteers, he struggled to get weapons and less than half were armed.

The smaller underground groups merged with the Union in the spring of 1940, anticipating an offensive by the Allies in the west.

But the defeat of France and the withdrawal of British troops to England in June came as shock to everyone in Poland and Brigadier-General Stefan Rowecki, (codename Rakon and Dart) moved the Union's headquarters to Warsaw.

The Gestapo used spies and informers to accumulate information on the Union and in 1941 it moved in to arrest soldiers and seize arms and funds. Some members were tortured into exposing their comrades, and the organization was left short of senior personnel.

The Home Army

The Union was renamed the Home Army (*Armia Krajowa,* AK) in February 1942 and the other underground groups transferred their members to it over time. Krakow's Home Army command was codenamed Crocodile and it was divided into four sections codenamed Woodpecker, Peafowl, Raven and Stork; they were later renamed Cement, Concrete, Granite and Lime.

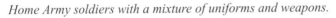

Home Army soldiers with a mixture of uniforms and weapons.

The Home Army had grown to around 350,000 members by the summer of 1944 and the Krakow Region alone had 90,000 soldiers. But running the Home Army in Krakow was a complicated and dangerous affair. The city was smaller than Warsaw and there were far more Germans, many who worked for the government, the military and the police. There were also a large number of informers operating across the city.

A Gestapo raid in the summer of 1944 struck lucky when it captured a list of thousands of decorated officers and non-commissioned officers. Although the names were encoded, it did not take the Gestapo code-breakers long to break it and many arrests followed.

Politically Motivated Military Organizations

Political groups also organized underground military organizations with the long term objective of taking over Poland once it had been liberated. The rural Peasant Party formed the Peasant Guards in 1941 and they were later converted into Peasant Battalions, under Franciszek Kamiński's command. The Battalions recruited in the countryside and fought to protect their communities. The number of members around the Krakow area grew to over 23,500 and they transferred to the Home Army in 1943.

Members of the National Party's National Military Organization made the mistake of using their own names while living at home. Once the Security Service discovered the group, the leaders were soon arrested. Major Wladyslaw Owoc arrived in July 1940 and he kept one step ahead of the Gestapo by changing addresses and working under his codename Paul and Fruktus. They codenamed the region *Ugory* while Krakow was codenamed *Krajewski*. On 20 September 1942 part of the National Military Organization merged with the radical Lizard Union Military Organization to form the National Armed Forces. However, recruitment was slow and Owoc offered his 700 members to the Home Army in July 1943.

Polish communists formed the Polish Workers' Party (PPR) in January 1942 and the Krakow region formed its own group. They established the People's Guard, a military organization later called the People's Army. The Polish communists pretended to fight for national liberation but they were pursuing communist objectives with Moscow's approval.

It did not take long for the Gestapo to infiltrate the Krakow Worker's Party, arrest many of its members and close it down. It did not re-emerge until the Red Army entered the city. Even so the Home Army's Bureau of Information and Propaganda started countering Communist and Soviet propaganda at the end of 1943 under Operation 'R'.

Assassinations

In the early days of the occupation, soldiers retrieved weapons and ammunition from hidden and abandoned caches. But they were soon exhausted and they had to steal from soldiers or police officers, usually after killing them. Underground members also robbed armaments from stores and some weapons were bought through the black market or from corrupt soldiers; money was sometimes raised by robbing the occasional bank.

An underground weapons factory (nicknamed the Insurance Company) was set up across Krakow in the summer of 1942. While some weapons were smuggled into the area, hundreds of Sten sub-machine guns were made in an agricultural machinery plant at 97 Mogilska. Grenade manufacture was spread across the city in dozens of apartments and around 50,000 grenades had been made by the time *SS-Oberführer* Walther Bierkamp arrested many of the Insurance Company employees in the spring of 1944.

The Home Army also had strike units which carried out attacks and sabotage. They came under the codename Lightning; followed by Thunderbolt, Jump and Hurricane and were led by Major Ian Panczakiewicz (codename Rock).

The assassination of high-ranking government officials and informers was a high priority. The Union for Armed Struggle had formed the Union for Retaliation in 1940 to track down, put on trial and execute informers and it became part of the Home Army's *Directorate of Subversion* (codename Kedyw). In May 1942 the Home Army formed the Special Combat Actions Organization, under

Colonel Jozef Szajewski (codename Philips). The assassination teams were codenamed Osa, the Polish word for 'wasp', and its members planned attacks against high-ranking offers.

Lieutenant Edward Madej (codename Felek) led the Krakow squads, (codename Kraw Gobelinie) and they attempted to shoot German officials (codenamed Heads) listed by the Directorate of Civil Resistance. High on the list was the General Government SS and Police Leader *SS-Obergruppenführer* Wilhelm Krüger. On 20 April 1943 Tadeusz Battek (codename Mountaineer) and Andrzej Jankowski (codename Strong Man) threw grenades at his car on Krasinskiego, seriously injuring him. Stanislaw Leopold (codename Rafal) planned to shoot Krüger's deputy, *SS-Obergruppenführer* Wilhelm Koppe, with a sniper rifle as he was driven from Wawel Castle. He made the attempt after cancelling the attack twice, but only injured Koppe's assistant.

Hans Frank was top of the assassination list and on 29 January 1944 Ryszard Nuszkiewicz (codename Slow) placed explosives on the railway track near Grodkowice, twelve miles east of Krakow. The explosion derailed the Governor-General's slow moving train and several Germans were injured in the gun-battle that followed. Hans Frank was unharmed but one hundred Poles were executed in retaliation. No more attacks were made on his life.

Major Panczakiewicz merged the strike teams into the Autonomous Partisan Battalion on 10 August 1944, in readiness for the anticipated uprising which never came.

Non-Violent Sabotage

A range of methods were used to undermine German morale, ranging from painting over German posters, to printing fake official letters, and to spreading propaganda and rumours by word-of mouth. In 1941 Tadeusz Zenczykowski (codename Kite and Nuthatch) organized the Bureau of Information and Propaganda and it printed over one million pieces of counter-propaganda under Codename 'N'. The Polish Scouting Association, an underground youth organization nicknamed the 'Grey Ranks', distributed the newsletters and put up posters across Krakow.

The Polish underground told people to boycott the cinema because ticket receipts were being forwarded to the Wehrmacht. They also sabotaged cinemas by pouring acid and other unpleasant products onto the seats to put cinema-goers off. Occasionally they would interrupt a film by releasing foul-smelling gas in the auditorium. The underground took their sabotage a step further on 9 September 1943 when their members started fires in four cinemas.

Planned Uprising

The Home Army planned around seventy attacks on headquarters, barracks and warehouses across Krakow during the spring of 1944, as part of a nationwide uprising called Operation Tempest. Unfortunately, Colonel Jozef Spychalski (codename February) was arrested in March 1944 and Lieutenant Colonel Wojciech Wayda (codename Revenge) managed the planning until Colonel Edward Godlewski (codename Guard) took over in July.

On 25 July everyone was put on standby, checking their weapons and explosives and making sure they had their red-and-white armbands marked 'WP' (for *Wojsko Polskie*, the Polish Army). The Polish Red Cross alerted their medical personnel and set up field

The Home Army armband.

hospitals ready to help the injured. Soldiers' families began stockpiling food and some even sent their children to stay with relatives.

Then on 1 August came news that the Home Army in Warsaw had gone on the offensive. The Germans expected something similar in Krakow and began fortifying the government district. General Heinrich Kittel took over the city on 5 August and ordered military units onto the streets. A few enthusiastic youngsters attacked the German soldiers on hearing about the uprising but nothing else happened. Some senior police officers wanted to carry out punitive arrests and executions to entice the people into an uprising but Governor-General Frank opposed the idea.

Meanwhile, Operational Group Krakow was still waiting for mobilization orders from Warsaw but it was difficult to get messages through. On 18 August General Count Tadeusz Komorowski (codename Forest) asked Godlewski if it would be possible to capture Krakow. The answer was a definite no. While the Home Army had 12,000 members in the city, only one in three were trained soldiers and only one in ten had a weapon. The Warsaw uprising ended on 2 October, ending any hopes of anything similar in Krakow.

Couriers, Radios and Newspapers

Wanda Marokini, codename 'Jadwiga' (the name of a famous fourteenth century Polish queen), ran a ring of couriers who carried instructions and money to hideouts and drop-off points. She organized them from 1 Pomorska, right across the street from the Gestapo headquarters. Wanda was arrested in May 1941 and held in Montelupich where she took poison, but failed to kill herself. She spent the rest of the war in Ravensbrück concentration camp which she miraculously survived. She died in 1962.

The Germans confiscated private radios early on and anyone caught listening to one was arrested; listening to a foreign station was a particularly heinous crime. In 1943 the Regional Government Delegation established a radio station codenamed *Wisia* on the south side of Krakow and kept in contact with London and Warsaw. The Germans monitored the frequency in an attempt to locate the radio equipment, but volunteers made sure it was moved regularly.

The White Eagle Organization had launched the weekly newspaper *Imperatives of the Day* in November 1939 and it contained news taken from foreign radio broadcasts; it soon had a circulation of 3,000.

The Polish Victory Service and the Union for Armed Struggle published 317 issues of the *Information Bulletin* during the occupation. By the time the Union became the Home Army in February 1942, there were over thirty regular publications in Krakow alone. Single sheet bulletins were also printed and women and schoolgirls carried them to drop-off points in apartment blocks and churches so others could distribute them. Railwaymen took them on their trains so they could be read in outlying villages. The appearance of a spoof copy of the German *Krakow Messenger* which mocked the General-Government was welcomed across the city.

The security services did what they could to shut printing presses down and twenty-one people were executed and another eighty deported when one was discovered on 28 July 1943. It was important that the editors, printers, couriers and distributors did not meet each other, so they could not betray others under torture.

Underground Theatre

The Krakow Underground Theatre had its opening night with the *Laughter is the Best Medicine* on 19 September 1940 and the young Adam Mularczyk staged more shows at 1 Zbrojow. Mieczyslaw Kotlarczyk opened the Rhapsodic Theatre on 1 November 1941 on Tyniecka and Karol Wojtyla was one of the actors; he would be the future Pope John Paul II from 1978 to 2005. Tadeusz Kantor founded the Underground Independent Theatre, Wieslaw Gorecki established the One-Actor Theatre and Tadeusz Kudlinski set up Studio 39. Tadeusz Kwiatkowski started publishing the *Literary*

Karol Wojtyla was ordained as a priest in November 1946.

Monthly magazine in November 1942 only to be arrested and held in Montelupich prison for several weeks in the summer of 1943.

Underground Punishments

The underground organization could be as ruthless as the Gestapo when it came to dealing with traitors, spies and informers. The Underground Resistance Judicial Commissions dealt with minor civilian cases, and punishments ranged from flogging to the shaving of women's heads. The Special Military Courts disciplined members of the underground army. Special Courts tried serious cases, and could impose the death penalty and published their name in the underground press.

The German authorities had little interest in protecting the Polish and the underground police stepped in when the 800 German-appointed Polish policemen failed to deal with crime across the city. They investigated murders and robberies and stopped extortion and muggings. The Community Guards maintained public order, the Citizens' Guards dealt with military order, and the State Security Corps trained personnel. While the numbers of underground police increased to 2,000, they only had around 75 guns to share between them.

The two most hated people in Krakow were the collaborator and the informer. Maurycy Diamand headed a group of Jewish informers until it was uncovered and its members executed in August 1944. Only Diamand escaped; his fate is not known.

Occasionally, captured underground members broke under interrogation and turned on their former comrades. They were released from prison so they could return to their group and report on their activities. Others who had turned were escorted around town in disguise, so they could point out their comrades to their handler.

Chapter 7

Moving into the Ghetto

Over the winter of 1940-41 all the Jews living in Krakow had to move out of their homes and into the Podgórze ghetto on the south bank of the Vistula. It was a major upheaval for them all as they were jammed into tiny, overcrowded apartments.

Making Lists

German soldiers had attacked Jewish businesses and people, particularly Orthodox Jews, since they entered Krakow. But anti-Semitic laws were planned and the General Government's Higher SS and Police Leaders met in Krakow on 8 November to agree that one million people (including 350,000 Jews) would have to be resettled over the winter.

A census began in Krakow the same day and the names of 68,482 Jews were gathered over the next two weeks. On 1 December 1939 every Jew aged twelve years and over had to wear a white band with a blue Star of David on their right arm, marking them for abuse.

Four days later the Kazimierz district, the main Jewish area on the south side of the old town, was sealed off by German troops. Everyone was ordered onto the streets and over the next twenty-four hours their apartments were searched for money, valuables and luxury household items. The banks were ordered to stop all accounts, freeze all savings and hold all safety deposit boxes belonging to Jews. Their limit on weekly withdrawals was set at 250 zloty and maximum anyone could hold was 2,000 zloty.

Decrees concerning work were announced on 26 October 1939 and while most Jews were restricted to manual and menial tasks, the higher professions, including lawyers, doctors and dentists, could only work with Jewish clients. All Jews between the age of twelve and sixty had to participate in compulsory public works, and they had to be available on Saturdays and other Jewish holidays.

Entering the Ghetto

Jews had already been banned from parks but they were prohibited from walking on many main streets on 30 April 1940, restricting their movements. The authorities then announced they wanted the capital to be the 'cleanest city' of the General Government. In other words they wanted to remove the Jews. On 15 August came the order the Jewish community had been dreading; only 15,000 workers and their families could live in the city. Around 50,000 had to leave the city and go and live elsewhere. The Jewish Council worked with the Department for Internal Affairs' Resettlement Commission, deciding who could stay and who had to go.

Few left to begin with, even though they could take as much luggage as they wanted. Then the SS and railway administrators started to work together and the police escorted the Jews to the stations while the *Ostbahn* organized the trains. The number of deportations increased to 8,000 a month and this time the Jews were limited to hand luggage. It was soon clear there were still over 15,000 too many in the city and the round-ups began on 29 November as the Police went through the addresses on the census and escorted everyone to a Displaced Persons camp on Mogilska, in the eastern suburbs. They were loaded onto cattle trucks and taken east to Lublin, Hrubieszow and Biala Podlaska; some ended up in the Warsaw ghetto.

Numbers dropped to 4,000 a month over the winter but by February 1941 the authorities demanded a rate of 15,000 a month. What they did not know was the Jewish Council had paid a German official called Reichert 100,000 zloty so another 10,000 Jews could stay in the city. On top of that, many deportees returned to the city having failed to find somewhere to live. Many would never return because they had been murdered in Belzec extermination camp.

On 3 March 1941 Chief of the Krakow District, *SS-*

Entering the ghetto via the Krakow Bridge.

Brigadeführer Dr Otto Wächter issued a directive establishing a new 'Jewish residential quarter' on the south bank of the River Vistula. Workers and their families were issued with new identification cards and a week later they were instructed to pack up their homes and move to the ghetto. Around 3,000 Polish residents had been moved out of Podgórze into former Jewish properties and they would be replaced by 15,000 Jews, creating massive overcrowding. Krakow's markets suddenly became busy with Jews selling their furniture and luxury items; they used the money to buy food.

The ghetto was in an unpleasant area of the city consisting of dilapidated nineteenth century tenements, most of them without a sewage system or running water. The district had only 3,167 rooms and Jewish Council's Housing Commission could only allocate two square metres of floor space per person. The regulations stipulated four families had to share one flat or a window for every three people. With so little space indoors, people spent a lot of time on the streets.

Everyone had to be inside the ghetto by 21 March and the official reasons given for the relocation were to improve policing and to reduce health risks. The unofficial reason was the General Government wanted to separate the Jewish community from the city's social and economic life. Ever the lawyer, Governor-General Hans Frank issued a decree *'on a controlled choice of the places of residence and stay by the Jewish people'* on 1 October; it legalized the relocation of 15,000 people into the ghetto.

No one could leave the ghetto without a pass and many continued to run their city centre shops until the Office for Economic Matters closed them down in July. They then had to watch as representatives of the Chamber of Industry and Commerce or the Chamber of Craftsmanship assessed their businesses at a fraction of their true value. They could not take anything into the ghetto and everything was sold at a knock-down price, with the money going to the Commercial Bank Corporation's 'forced displacement' account.

At the same time the Trusteeship Office employed experts to value property left in the abandoned Jewish apartments on behalf of the Office for Economic Matters. The Housing Office placed Polish families in them and the Furniture Management Office offered the contents for sale. All proceeds were paid into the city's Municipal Fund's 'foreign money' account.

Guarding the Ghetto
The ghetto was sealed on 21 March 1941 and German police officers supervised Polish and Jewish policemen as they patrolled the barbed wire perimeter. Notice boards with the rules were put up but they were all written in the Hebrew alphabet, which was only understood by a few learned men. It was a cynical move to catch people out so they could be punished.

The barbed wire was soon being replaced by brick walls and it did not go unnoticed that the Polish bricklayers shaped the top like a line of tombstones. Doors and ground-floor windows were bricked around the perimeter to make sure no one could sneak out. Before long the ghetto was surrounded by walls and there were only four guarded exits.

The Jews were only allowed to leave the ghetto to go to work while vehicles needed authorization to enter and the police checked

A tram passes through a gate in the ghetto wall.

everyone's passes. Delivery vehicles and refuse trucks used the main gate which opened onto Podgórze Market (Rynek Podgórze) at the west end of Limanowskiego St while pedestrians used a side gate. Many were marched through the north-east exit on Consent Square (Plac Zgody) as they headed off to work in the city. Those who worked for Oskar Schindler left by this gate and walked 400 metres along Kacik Street to the factory. Military units and vehicles entered the ghetto via the east gate, at the junction of Jozefinska Street and Lwowska Street. There was a fourth gate at the opposite end of Limanowskiego St, at the south-east corner of the ghetto. Trams ran along Limanowskiego St but they never stopped.

The Jewish Council

The Jewish Council took orders from the German authorities and saw that their community followed them. Marek Biberstein's council of elders was based in Podgórze town hall, on the corner of Podgorski Market and Limanowskiego St, next to the ghetto's main entrance.

While the fraud allowing extra Jews to stay in the city went unnoticed, the official called Reichert was also taking bribes from people in exchange for work permits, so they could stay in the city. An informer reported the corruption to the Gestapo and Reichert and five members of the Judenrat were arrested in the summer of 1941. Reichert was sentenced to eight years in prison, Biberstein was given eighteen months and his deputy Joachim Goldfluss six months. (After his release, Marek Biberstein was murdered in Plaszow camp in 1944.)

Dr Artur Rosenzweig was appointed the new head of the Judenrat and his team were kept busy carrying out the General Government's decrees and orders. They also had the difficult job of distributing rations and bribed suppliers to deliver extra food into the ghetto, sometimes using refuse trucks to smuggle it in. Dr Maurycy Haber's Jewish Social Self-Help association (JSS) also paid for food to be smuggled in. Even kosher meat, which had been banned since 26 October 1939, was brought into the ghetto from a ritual butcher operating secretly in the city suburbs.

Despite the attempts to supplement the diet, living conditions deteriorated. The Sanitary Commission struggled to control hygiene

The Judenrat's offices.

in an area where the sewage system was overwhelmed and the refuse trucks could not cope with the mountains of rubbish. But despite the insanitary conditions and a lack of soap and cleaning products, the ghetto remained free of contagious diseases.

The Jewish Order Service

The Germans did not want to deploy their own police inside the ghetto so they employed Jewish men to keep order. They gave them passes so they and their families could enter and leave the ghetto; it meant they could buy and barter for food. The *Jewish Order Service* (OD) was organized by the Judenrat following a Gestapo order issued on 5 July 1940. The Order Service chief was Symche Spira and his headquarters were at 17 Jozefinska Street, at its junction with Krakusa Street. The building had holding cells and prisoners were forwarded to Montelupich Prison or to Auschwitz concentration camp; some were later executed in Plaszow labour camp.

The original group of OD police were sociable men, chosen for their community skills. But Spira relished the Gestapo's orders and had soon replaced them with yes men who accepted bribes. They wore a cap and an armband as their uniform and often acted as auxiliaries for the German police. They did the tasks the Germans did not want to do, carrying out searches and clearing apartments. They also ran a ring of informers and arrested anyone caught breaking the ghetto rules.

Community Assistance

The Jewish Social Self-Help association (JSS) had been established in May 1940 as an agency of the Superior Welfare Council (*Naczelna Rada Opiekuncza*, NRO). The head of the city's JSS, Michal Weichert, moved into the Krakow ghetto in March 1941 and he opened an office at 18 Jozefinska. The NRO accepted food, medicines and clothes from many sources and the JSS distributed them. Donations came from the General Government, the International Red Cross, Jewish charity organizations (mainly based in Sweden and Switzerland) and from the American Jewish Joint Distribution Committee (nicknamed the Joint). The JSS also bought foodstuffs and medical supplies on the black market. The Talmud's rule of 'Just Conduct' stated that Jewish believers should donate a fifth of their property to charity to compensate for their sins and the JSS held Sunday street collections.

Dr Weichert cooperated with the Germans to get the best for the poor but some thought he was too cooperative. Underground organizations sentenced him to death, a threat that was never carried out, and while he was put on trial after the war he was acquitted and exonerated.

Despite the difficulties, the community leaders worked hard to run facilities which helped the weaker members of society. Women and their daughters worked in the three kitchens to make soup from the small amounts of potatoes and bread available.

Dr Jozef Nissenfeld and Dr Maksymilian Blassberg ran a community hospital on Skawinska and on 31 October 1941 they moved it to 14 Jozefinska. The hospital dealt with patients from the ghetto and neighbouring towns and Polish doctors helped out during busy times. Dr Jakub Kranz opened an infirmary for the disabled and elderly at 15 Limanowskiego while Professor Julian Aleksandrowicz and Dr Bernard Bornstein ran a hospice at 10 Jozefinska. Dr Aleksander Biberstein also opened an isolation hospital for patients with infectious diseases in a closed down Jewish school at 30 Rekawka. Showers, baths, steam baths, ritual baths and disinfection equipment were set up at 3 Jozefinska to help control the spread of diseases.

Anna and Leopold Feuerstein moved the Roia Rockowa Centre for Jewish Orphans to 8 Krakusa in May 1941 and they were assisted by Rachela Ehrlich, Rozalia Kreppel, and Dawid Kurzmann. The Trade Boarding School for Orphans was set up at 35 Jozefinska.

The Eagle Pharmacy
The Polish run Eagle Pharmacy (*Apteka Pod Orlem*) stood at the south-west corner of Consent Square. Tadeusz Pankiewicz and his three assistants, Irena Droidzikowska, Aurelia Danek Czortowa and Helena Krywaniuk, worked to keep it open twenty-four hours a day, seven days a week, selling medical supplies to the people. Pankiewicz

paid bribes to keep his pharmacy open and helped as many as he could, in spite of the risks. The building became a meeting place where news was exchanged and rumours were shared but it was also a place to pass on messages so Pankiewicz's staff could smuggle them in and out of the ghetto.

Working

The Labour Office at 10 Jozefinska allocated jobs and there were always queues of men outside hoping for work, so they could avoid the round-ups and selections. Workers were lined up in Consent Square and either marched or driven away, escorted by a Works Protection unit, to their place of employment. Many worked on the Zablocie industrial estate, making everything from radiators to crates and barrack components. Some worked in Plaszow, in the Liban quarries and Schindler's enamelware factory; others worked at

A map of the Krakow ghetto.

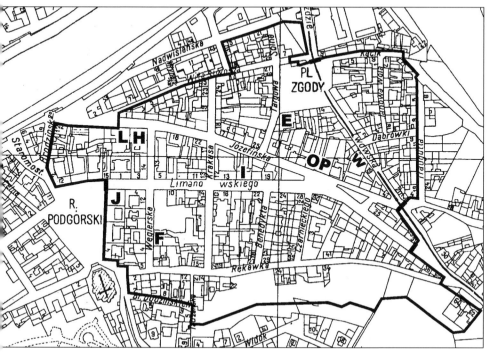

Key
E Eagle Pharmacy	I Infirmary	O Orphanage
F Optima Factory	J Judenrat Offices	P OD Police Station
H Hospital	L Labour Office	W Ghetto Wall

Bonarka's brickworks or in the warehouses on Rakowice airfield. Others were employed cleaning the city streets, on the railways or in the Gestapo workshops on Pomorska Street; a few worked for the General Government in Wawel Castle.

Some people worked in the food shops, hairdressers, dentists, tailors, launderettes, cafes and restaurants in the ghetto. Feliks Dziuba was the only Pole operating a business inside its walls making glasses for an army contractor at 6 Targowa. Everyone had to take part in menial community tasks once a week, be it sweeping the streets, cleaning up the green spaces or clearing snow.

Workers were paid a minimum wage in the early days and then they were unpaid. Working conditions depended very much on the employer's attitude to Jews but they were exempt from all regulations relating to working hours, contracts and safety.

Teaching and Religion

The Germans believed the Jews should be uneducated but community leaders believed every student should learn about their religion and culture and also master a profession. Young children were taught in the backyard of the Optima factory at 9 Wegierska while older students were taught in secret classes.

Orthodox Jews did their best to follow their religious practices and some adhered to ritual fast days even though they were banned. The Jewish Council had to order men to cut their beards and hair to avoid harassment. People could attend one of the three synagogues, the Bikur Cholim Synagogue at 13 Limanowskiego, the Zucker Synagogue at 5 Wegierska, and the Skawina Synagogue at 3 Jozefinska.

Shabbat is the weekly Jewish feast which starts at sunset on Friday and lasts to sunset on Saturday. Jews were supposed to spend the time resting, attending the synagogue, studying the Torah and celebrating with their families. However, everyone was made to work and Saturdays were a favourite time to search the ghetto.

Entertainment

The ghetto newspaper, *Gazeta Zydowska*, organized a small orchestra at 4 Dabrowskiego and appealed for people to hand over their spare musical instruments. It held regular charity concerts at the Trade Boarding School at 39 Jozefinska. A concert hall was opened on 25 February 1942 in a former chocolate factory at 9 Wegierska but the concerts were stopped at the end of May, following a large round-up. But the music continued and the Rosner Players, led by Leo Rosner, performed a concert at the OD police station on 16 August.

People sometimes spent their free time on Krzemionki Hill, the only green place in the ghetto. It was a busy place on a Sunday as men talked, women chatted and youngsters flirted. The only other area of grass was a small open space on Jozefinska and it too became busy when it was sunny.

The Deportations Start

In the autumn of 1941, Krakow's chief of police, *Stadthauptmann* Rudolf Pavlu, issued a directive ordering 6,000 Jews to move from outlying towns and villages into the ghetto. The Jewish community leaders tried in vain to acquire new apartment blocks and there were frantic times as they made space for the new comers. The deadline was set for 1 October, Yom Kippur, the Day of Atonement, one of the most important days in the Jewish calendar. It had been chosen to humiliate the Jews and rather than spending the day in prayer in their synagogue, thousands of people queued for hours in the snow outside the ghetto walls.

The overcrowding became unbearable and at the end of November the chief of police issued orders to begin deportations. The OD police went to work dragging 1,000 people from their rooms and taking them to the railway station, ready to be taken in cattle trucks to Lublin. A few days later another 1,000 people were rounded up.

The chief of police issued a new directive on 27 December, calling for all fur coats and other fur products to be handed in. Many burnt, dumped or cut up their furs in disgust rather than having them confiscated. German and Polish policemen then searched the ghetto the following day, taking the opportunity to remove all the luxury goods and food people had saved for Hannukkah, the Jewish Festival of Light.

Chapter 8

Closing the Ghetto

The Wannsee Conference and Operation Reinhard
Following the invasion of the Soviet Union on 22 June 1941, *Reichsführer-SS* Heinrich Himmler began studying how to realize the Final Solution of the Jewish question (*Endlösung der Judenfrage*). *Reichsmarschall* Hermann Göring also instructed Himmler's deputy, *SS-Gruppenführer* (later *SS-Obergruppenführer*) Reinhard Heydrich to submit practical plans for deporting and murdering Europe's Jews, on behalf of the Reich Main Security Office.

On 16 December 1941 he made it clear that the Jews had no future in the General Government:

> *"Let me make it openly clear to you, Gentlemen; the Jews must be done away with, be it this way or another... In January a major conference is planned in Berlin for that matter, to which I shall delegate State Secretary Dr Josef Bühler... Anyway, a mass migration of Jews is expected... Gentlemen, you must force back all the milk of human kindness in you. We must destroy the Jews wherever we come across them, and wherever we can, in order to maintain the general structures of the Reich here."*

The meeting he was referring to was chaired by Heydrich on 20 January 1942 at a villa in Wannsee, near Berlin. There he told government state secretaries his plans for what would become known as the Holocaust. After months of arbitrary killing by the *Einsatzgruppen*, the extermination of the Jews was going to be organized on an industrial scale. Heydrich, aided by Jewish expert

SS-Obersturmbannführer Adolf Eichmann, explained that there would be no more Jewish emigration, instead they would be deported to the East and evacuated; a euphemism for murder. Another euphemism used was 'Special Treatment' (*Sonderbehandlung*); it too meant murder.

Heydrich wanted the department heads to cooperate in the deportation of European Jews by train to extermination camps in the General Government area. There they would be separated into the fit who would be worked to death and the elderly, the children and the sick who would be murdered in gas chambers. The plan was to eliminate Europe's Jewish communities as quickly as possible and the deportations would begin straight away. Hans Frank asked Dr Bühler to make it clear he wanted to start with the General Government's overcrowded ghettos.

New extermination camps were set up in the General Government area over the winter of 1941-42. The first one at Chelmno, thirty miles north of Lódź, had murdered its first transport of Jews on 8 December 1941. Belzec camp, between Lublin and Lviv, and Sobibor, north-east of Lublin, opened next followed by Treblinka, north-east of Warsaw. The ghettos across the General Government deported all their 'surplus Jewish labour', the euphemism for those unable to work, in the summer of 1942. Around eighty per cent were murdered in the gas chambers as part of *Aktion Reinhard*; possibly named after Reinhard Heydrich, who had been assassinated by the Czech Resistance in Prague in May 1942.

Relocating Krakow's Jews to Plaszow Camp
Krakow's ghetto was overcrowded by the spring of 1942 and the threat of typhus rose as the warm weather approached. On 29 May everyone was instructed to report to the Jewish Social Self-Help offices at 18 Jozefinska. Over the next three days Gestapo officers checked identification cards and Employment Office officials stamped those engaged in essential work; their family members were also given stamps. The OD police assembled everyone without a stamp in Zgody Square and told them they were going to be leaving the ghetto and they could only take hand luggage and 25 zloty.

Plac Zgody's police station; the chairs represent those taken from the ghetto.

On 1 June those with a job left for work and then the OD police rounded up 2,000 people without a stamp in Zgody Square. The Germans blamed Artur Rosenzweig, head of the Jewish Council, for failing to gather more and he and his family had to join those waiting to leave. Later that afternoon they were marched to Plaszow railway station and loaded into cattle vans, never to be seen again. The ID checks continued for two nights and anyone who refused to cooperate was beaten; a few were shot.

But the Germans were losing their patience. On 4 June 1942 Armed Special Service units (*Sonderdienst*), supported by the Polish police and Construction Service workers (*Baudienst*), entered the ghetto after all those with a job had left. They carried out a thorough search of the apartment blocks, dragging everyone they found onto the streets, beating and shooting anyone who resisted. They took them all to Plaszow railway station and they were never seen again. The blood-stained streets were silent when the workers returned to the ghetto.

But the Germans had not finished. Two days later everyone had to report to the Jozefinska Employment Office with their identification cards (*Kennkarten*) so they could be given their work permit, known as the blue slip (*Blauschein*). Feliks Dziuba obtained blue slips for his workers from the director of the Jewish Labour Force so his factory could continue making glasses. An official called Szepessy was soon denounced for providing them and deported to a concentration camp.

Identification checks continued and everyone without a blue slip was taken to the Optima factory on Wegierska and searched for valuables. They were held in the yard for two days and then on 8 June they were marched two miles south-east to Prokocim railway station and loaded onto a waiting train. They too were never seen again.

On 10 June 1942 Higher SS and Police Leader Julian Scherner ended the action; 7,000 people had been sent to Belzec extermination camp and gassed. Back in the ghetto people spoke in hushed tones about the fate of their relatives and friends. The Germans had told them they were going to work in the Ukraine and everyone believed the lie to begin with. But a few weeks later, a Pole whose Jewish wife had been deported during the June actions said he had heard they had been gassed. The terrible news spread like wildfire around the ghetto. But while the story frightened people, they could not believe that the Germans were capable of planning and carrying out mass murder.

Reducing the Ghetto

On 20 June 1942 city governor *SS-Hauptsturmführer* Rudolf Pavlu told Dawid Gutter, the new head of the Jewish Council, that the ghetto had to be reduced by a further twenty per cent so the apartments south of Rekawka and the block on the east side of Podgórze Market Square could be turned over to Poles. They only had twenty-four hours to move.

The Judenrat also had to relocate to 16 Wegierska while the isolation hospital had to transfer its patients to 3 Zgody Square, an unsuitable building with no sewage system. The orphans moved to 31 Jozefinska only for the OD chief, Symche Spira, to order them to make way for his police two months later; they moved in with the older children at 41 Jozefinska. All the shops, workshops and firms in the requisitioned area had to move and the Jewish Craftsmen's

Association organized space for the community's tailors, seamstresses and cobblers in other buildings, including the Optima factory at 6 Wegierska.

Life was becoming unbearable for everyone but more so for some, particularly the elderly. A few desperate people offered to inform for the Gestapo in return for rewards. Others decided they could take no more and committed suicide, using gas or potassium cyanide as a poison. The deportations had frightened many, and some chose to carry poison so they could commit suicide rather than die at the hands of the Germans.

Reducing the Ghetto even further

By the autumn of 1942 plans were being drawn up to close the ghetto. On 27 October SS and Police Leader *SS-Oberführer* Julian Scherner issued a directive to build a labour camp on the site of two Jewish cemeteries in the Plaszow district, one mile south-east of the ghetto. Businesses and their workers would be moved to the camp while those who were unable to work would be deported to Belzec extermination camp.

Loudhailer announcements called for workers to gather at the Labour Office (*Arbeitsamt*) instead of the ghetto gate the following morning and a Gestapo officer spent several hours deciding who could leave for work. A few people had gone into hiding, fearing deportation and some parents used bromide to make their children sleep, so the OD men did not find their hiding places and take them to the orphanage.

The mood turned menacing when *SS-Sturmbannführer* Willi Haase led armed Special Service officers into the ghetto. Loudhailers called upon everyone to line up along Jozefinska, making it clear that anyone who disobeyed the order would be shot. As the SS and Special Service patrols searched the apartments, IDs were checked and the majority had to assemble in Zgody Square where Latvian and Lithuanian auxiliaries had set up machine guns on trestle tables.

Around midday all the patients were ordered out of the Jozefinska hospice. A few terminally ill were shot in their beds while those unable to walk were hauled away on horse-drawn wagons. The

Marching those who cannot work to the transports.

elderly and disabled patients in the Limanowskiego infirmary were taken into the building's backyard and shot, alongside the director Doctor Jakub Kranz.

The same happened in the yard of the Jozefinska orphanage while soldiers threw a few children out of the windows so others could shoot at them. Anna and Leopold Peuerstein and Dawid Kurzmann had to lead the terrified older children to Zgody Square and then watch as they were escorted through the Wegierska gate. They were escorted to Plaszow railway station and taken by train to Belzec camp. Everyone else in the square soon followed as they too were led off to their deaths.

The seriously ill and the small children were taken by horse drawn wagons to Plaszow labour camp where graves had been dug. The adults were shot but the guards chose not to waste bullets on the children; they threw them into the pits and buried them alive.

When the workers returned to the ghetto around 6pm they were shocked to find the ghetto virtually deserted. There were bodies on the streets, apartments had been broken open and all that was left were farewell notes written by their loved ones.

The ghetto's Labour Office.

Around 4,500 Jews had been taken to Belzec camp and another 600 had been shot. Loudhailers then announced that everyone living in the east side of the ghetto had only twenty-four hours to relocate to the west side.

The Labour Office was then closed because the SS was taking over the employment of the Jews. Companies were told to submit lists of workers so the police could issue new work passes (*Judenpässe*) and they would pay the SS five zlotys per man per day and four zlotys per woman; the worker received nothing apart from a bowl of watery soup around midday.

A directive announced on 14 November 1942 stated Jews were only allowed to live in one of the five ghettos in the General Government area; Warsaw, Krakow, Lwow, Radom and Bochnia.

Every other town and village had to be 'cleansed of Jews' (*Judenrein*) by the end of the month. Jews were told they would be given jobs and left alone if they voluntarily moved into the ghettos. It was just another lie. As November came to a close hundreds of Jews moved into the empty apartments to find there was no work, leaving them reliant on the ghetto's soup kitchens for food.

On 6 December 1942 a barbed wire fence was erected along Jozefinska, creating Ghetto A for workers with passes and Ghetto B for those without. Ghetto A's children were kept in a day care centre on the corner of Krakusa and Jozefinska while Ghetto B's children stayed with their parents. A new orphanage was opened on Jozefinska.

Living Outside the Ghetto
A few Jews attempted to live outside the ghetto, knowing that one mistake would result in them and their helpers being executed. It was a life full of danger and they had to speak fluent Polish, follow Polish behaviour and customs, and had to look and dress correctly if they were to fit in.

Fugitives would have to buy the correct documents and then escape from the walled ghetto without being caught. They had to rely on strangers on the outside and most Poles were too afraid to help. Some took the risk in exchange for money but they would throw their 'guest' out as soon as their cash ran out. A few took pity and hid friends for free but they lived in fear of being reported by their neighbours. The Germans offered rewards for denouncing hidden Jews and some people blackmailed those hiding people.

Attempts to help Jews in hiding were organized by Tadeusz Seweryn, head of the Civil Resistance in the Krakow Region. His team worked to punish collaborators and execute Gestapo informers and blackmailers. In February 1943 he was instructed to establish the 'Council to Aid Jews' (*Zegota,* RPZ) and its first meeting was held on 12 March 1943, only one day before the Germans started liquidating the Krakow ghetto. The Krakow branch did what they could to help the Jews organize resistance, provided them with false passes so they could move freely. In February 1944 the Polish

Government in Exile set up an investigation department in Krakow to assist the Civil Resistance in its work.

Resistance in the Ghetto

Despite the risks, some young Jews were determined to organize sabotage and assassinations. In August 1942 the *Akiva* youth organization and the *Dror* socialist organization amalgamated into the Fighting Pioneer Youth Organization (*He-Chalutz*) under Shimson Dränger, Adolf Liebeskind and Abraham Leibowicz (codename Laban). A month later they were joined by a group called Spark (*Iskra*) and changed their title to the Jewish Combat Organization (*Zydowska Organizacja Bojowa*, ZOB).

On 21 November 1942 ZOB's leaders met for a Shabbat supper at 13 Jozefinska in what would later be called the organization's 'last supper'. Dolek Liebeskind wanted action and said *"we are fighting for three lines in history, so that it would never be claimed that our nation was driven to slaughter like cattle."* Two days later he and two other men murdered a German policeman and stole his gun. The Germans retaliated by arresting twenty people and deported them to Auschwitz; Dolek's wife Ewa was among them. The following day the ZOB leaders agreed they should go to their hideouts and await further instructions.

Yitzhak Zuckerman and Havka Polman delivered orders to start an uprising from Warsaw on 22 December 1942. The same evening girls scattered leaflets, put up posters and hung Polish flags in the Debnicki district of the city. They also laid wreaths at Adam Mickiewicz's monument (a Polish national poet) and where a plaque commemorating a Polish uprising of 1794 had once been.

Several attacks were made and a grenade killed eleven people and injured thirteen in the German Cyganeria café on Szpitalna. The ZOB members then headed back to the ghetto to start an uprising; unfortunately two Jewish collaborators made sure the Gestapo stopped it happening.

A trap had been set at the Jewish hospital on Skawinska St and while Yitzak Zuckerman escaped injured, Leibowicz was arrested. His interrogation led the Secret Police to Adolf Liebeskind and Iuda

Tennenbaum and they were shot dead at their hideout. Many other men and women were rounded up and Szymon Dränger was arrested on 10 January 1943. His wife Gusta handed herself in to the Gestapo in an act of solidarity; both were later released.

The surviving members of ZOB moved to Bochnia, twenty-five miles east of Krakow, in February 1943 and joined Hilel Wodzislawski's group. Their move must have been compromised because all but Wodzislawski were arrested on 13 March 1943. Wodzislawski was finally caught and shot in October 1943. Dränger was re-arrested on 8 November 1943 and he told his interrogators where his wife was hiding so they could fulfil their vow to die together. By the end of 1943, the Jewish Combat Association was finished in the Krakow area.

Theirs was not the only act of defiance. Twenty Jewesses made a break from Helclow St when they realized they were going to be executed on 29 April 1943. While some were killed and the majority were caught and shot, two escaped.

Liquidating the Ghetto

SS-Untersturmführer Amon Göth was appointed commandant of Plaszow labour camp on 11 February 1943 and he immediately put plans together to prepare for the ghetto's closure. Construction work was stepped up ready to accept the Jews and in early March he told the Jewish Council to relocate working Jews from Ghetto A. But the relocation progressed slowly; Göth became impatient and decided to close the ghetto quickly using force.

Early on the morning of 13 March Plaszow's SS and Ukrainian guards (who were known as 'blacks' due to the colour of their uniforms) surrounded the ghetto and stopped everyone leaving for work. The Jews waited nervously and then at 11am announcements instructed all workers to gather at the Wegierska gate with their Judenpasses and hand luggage, ready to leave in two hours.

The ghetto was then plunged into chaos as Göth, his staff and a group of fearsome dogs led the camp guards through the streets. OD men shouted orders, adults ran about searching for their families and children cried. Whistles, barking, shouting and gunshots echoed

The ghetto hospital.

through the narrow streets as the guards dragged people from their apartments, shooting anyone who got in their way. Some hid their children, hoping to return later, but many youngsters wandered the streets looking for their parents.

As those with passes were lined up by the gate, the rest were moved into Ghetto B with false promises of work. Doctors gave those too ill to move in the hospitals lethal doses of drugs. Mothers were told to leave their small children behind, with assurances they would be brought to the camp later. No one believed the promises and while some stayed, others lined up with their children hidden in their backpacks or under their coats. Few reached the camp.

The camp guards then escorted the columns of Jews to Plaszow, beating anyone who could not keep up. By the early afternoon the only people left in Ghetto A were the Jewish Council, the OD-men, a few children in the nursery and those who had gone into hiding.

The guards now turned their attentions to Ghetto B where the unemployed, the elderly, children and those who decided to stay with their children waited in fear. They conducted the same terrifying round-up, only this time they escorted everyone to the railway station. The following day transports carried 2,000 to Birkenau where 1,500 were sent straight to the gas chambers.

Krakow ghetto was left silent; the scattered bodies and suitcases on the streets, testament to the chaotic and brutal liquidation. Around 2,000 had been murdered and one of the first jobs was to load the corpses onto horse-drawn carts while others dug mass graves in Plaszow camp.

Jewish work parties spent the summer preparing the ghetto area ready for Poles to move in. Furniture and household goods were cleaned and repaired while clothes were mended. German books were resold while all Polish and Jewish literature was torn up and sold as scrap paper. High value art items were shipped to Germany, low value pieces were put on sale and Jewish art was burnt. Only the synagogue's Torah scrolls were saved and they were hidden in the Eagle Pharmacy (Tadeusz Pankiewicz handed them to Krakow's Jewish Historical Commission after the war).

The apartments were then cleaned and renovated, removing all traces of the violent liquidation. The walls and barbed wire fences were also taken down, removing the final traces of the ghetto. In December 1943 hundreds of Polish families were moved into the tiny Podgórze apartments. They too had to sell or abandon the possessions they could not take with them and they were either sold or rented to the Germans who took over the houses the Poles had left.

Chapter 9

The Oskar Schindler Story

Oskar Schindler was born on 28 April 1908 in Zwittau in Czechoslovakia, some 100 miles east of Prague (the town is now called Svitavy and is in the Czech Republic). He had a good relationship with his mother Franziska (Fanny) and younger sister Elfriede but he did not get on with his father, Hans Schindler. Oskar was not a diligent student and while he went to college in Brno to study business and machine engineering, he was more interested in girls, drinking and fighting.

Oskar Schindler.

After trying to work for his father's agricultural machinery company for a time, 21-year-old Schindler turned to sales to make a living, topping up his income with gambling. He met his future wife, Emilie Pelzl, in the autumn of 1927 and they married the following spring without their parents consent.

Around 1936 Schindler joined the German Sudeten Party (SdP) and chose to work for the German military intelligence organization, the *Abwehr*. His work allowed him to travel into Poland and report on the Polish Army and fortifications, and he also travelled to Krakow, a city he would get to know very well. In 1938 the couple relocated to Moravska Ostrava, on the Polish border, and their house became a contact point for agents spying on Poland.

Then the Czechoslovakian police arrested Schindler on 18 July 1938 on charges of espionage and anti-Czech activity, treasonable offences which carried the death penalty. Fortunately for Schindler, the Munich Agreement was signed on 30 September 1938, annexing the Sudetenland to the Third Reich. Prisoners of German nationality were released under the Agreement, so Oskar was free to go, but he was unable to enter into what remained of Czechoslovakia.

The German Sudeten Party was incorporated into the National Socialist German Workers' Party (NSDAP) in February 1939 and Schindler automatically became a member. He continued on his sales travels around Poland, reporting what he saw, as diplomacy between Nazi Germany and the Soviet Union meant the invasion of Poland was imminent.

While Schindler was gaining experience as a salesman, three Jewish industrialists, Michal Gutman, Wolf Glajtman and Izrael Kohn, were looking to invest in a new venture in Krakow. They became partners of the *Rekord Factory* on 17 March 1937, which they advertised as the *First Enamelware and Tinware Factory in Lesser Poland* (the historical region covering part of southern Poland). The factory was located at 4 Lipowa and they sold their products from a rented shop at nearby 9 Romanowicza. Glajtman's brother-in-law, Abraham Bankier, joined the board but the business did not flourish and hit financial problems after only two years. The partners filed for bankruptcy in June 1939.

Schindler Comes to Krakow

The Wehrmacht entered Krakow on 6 September and Schindler arrived on the 7th, one of many businessmen looking to make money. He was soon discussing how to rent a confiscated Jewish firm from its German administrators. To begin with he became director of a small workshop at 52 Krakowska, which put him in contact with Abraham Bankier, former owner of the Rekord Factory. After speaking to Izaak Stern, Bankier's accountant, he worked out how to make more money by producing enamelware cooking utensils for the Wehrmacht. The paperwork arrived from the German Trusteeship Office on 14 November 1939, making him the new owner.

Schindler found lodgings at 24 Krasinskiego on the west side of the city but he soon moved to apartment 8 at 14 Sereno Fenna on the north side. He finally settled in apartment 2 at 7 Straszewskiego, a confiscated Jewish apartment within sight of Wawel Castle, the seat of the Nazi General Government.

The Factory Opens

The German Enamelware Factory (*Deutsche Emailwarenfabrik*, DEF) opened for business in January 1940 and Schindler was soon offering samples to army purchasers – only the samples had not been made in *Emalia* (as the factory was called). Schindler had spent 28,000 zloty on enamelled vessels and mess tins and was offering them as his own. He had also commissioned new offices, a kitchen with canteen and a clinic, using the money provided by the Jewish sponsors.

With contracts secured, the plant went into production with a work force of one hundred Poles and seven Jews. While Schindler entertained potential clients and did the deals, Izaak Stern, Abraham Bankier and Wolf Glajtman managed the plant.

The Emalia factory gates.

The factory started making galvanized mess tins for the army and the money started to roll in, so he invested in an extension to the shop floor and new sheet metal presses. A three-storey building was added to the front of the factory in 1942 with offices for the design, technical and administrative staff. Production switched to munitions as Schindler increased his military contracts and he finally settled on making shell casings in 1943. Schindler had new offices and sleeping quarters added. He also treated himself to a stable block for his beloved horses and a large garage for his fleet of cars.

The Workforce

The number of Jews increased, until 175 were working on Emalia's factory floor. But Schindler saw the financial advantage of employing more when the ghetto was established in March 1941. Poles were more expensive than the five zloty a day for men and four zloty for women the SS were charging for Jewish labour. The number of Jews in the factory rose to 550 in 1942, 900 in 1943, and about 1,100 in 1944. Over time they started to call themselves *Schindlerjuden* – Schindler's Jews.

Schindler with his workforce.

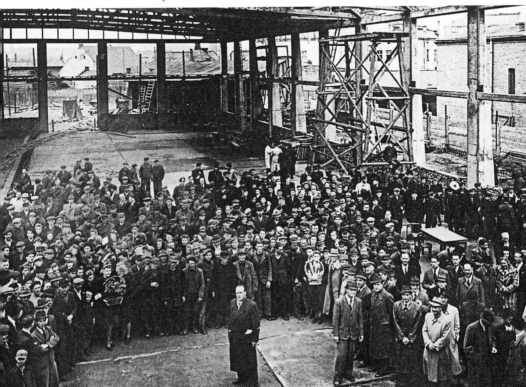

To begin with the works supervisor, Willi Schöneborn, organized two twelve-hour shifts but the working day was split into three eight-hour shifts when extra workers were taken on. He was rarely interrupted by the guards because Schindler banned them from the factory floor unless they had permission, saying they distracted the workers. He also used his contacts in the Wehrmacht and SS to get advance warnings about inspections and deportations, to keep his workers safe from selections.

Schindler had a mixed work force of men and women while a number of elderly people, some disabled and a few children worked under forged papers, keeping family groups together. They worked with Poles who shared news, they were fed more food and were given medical care. Above all, they were not subjected to the abuse and violence suffered by Plaszow's workers. Schindler's initial attitude to his workforce was to exploit them to make a profit, but he saw and heard enough over time to change his attitude.

But while some workers remember Schindler with gratitude and affection, not all did. They had to work long hours with dangerous machinery, hazardous chemicals and inadequate safety measures. There was no heating in the cold factory and barracks in the winter, and lice spread dysentery and typhus in the hot summer months.

A Sub-Camp of Plaszow

When Plaszow opened Schindler faced a choice. He could employ Poles and send his Jewish workforce to the camp, as other businesses in Krakow were doing, or build accommodation for his workers on site. His workers had walked to and fro from the ghetto to the factory every day, a distance of only 500 metres but the distance increased to over 1 mile if they moved to Plaszow. He would have also become aware of the brutality in the camp.

Schindler argued that the long walk exhausted his workforce, reduced production and made it difficult to meet his army contracts. Göth eventually agreed he could build a sub-camp in the Emalia factory, providing it met SS requirements. Money also changed hands to ease the transition.

In a matter of days barrack blocks, two watchtowers and a barbed wire fence had been built around a parade ground. Around 450 Jews moved in so they could work and sleep out of sight of passers-by. Three more barrack blocks were soon built next to the factory for another 558 workers; 174 of them for Emalia and the rest split between three other factories. The SS made sure the sub-camp complied with the security regulations and took payment; Schindler dealt with all queries.

On 8 May 1943 Emalia became a sub-camp of Plaszow with the official name *Jewish Forced Labour Camp of the SS and Police Commandant in the United Company of the German Enamelware Factory*. Workers had originally been sent by the Labour Office but Schindler dealt directly with Göth once Plaszow camp opened. His workers sometimes put in requests to transfer their families and friends to Emalia and Schindler arranged bribes for OD-man Marcel Goldberg so their names were put on the transfer papers.

SS-Oberscharführer Albert Hujar was Emalia's first commandant and he ran the sub-camp by the rule book, often flogging workers for minor infractions. Ukrainian guards patrolled the perimeter and plant guards were on call to keep order on the factory floor and take the roll calls. Perec Selinger's group of OD men did the leg work for the guards, organizing the roll calls and running the barracks.

Saving Other People

Dr Michal Weichert urged businessmen to donate money to Krakow's Jewish Aid Centre so he could buy food for forced labourers and Schindler allowed the Centre to distribute extra rations to his workforce. After February he allowed some of his workers to obtain supplies from the Council to Aid Jews (*Zegota*), a Polish underground organization. Schindler used to claim he had bought food on the black market if questioned and that he had done so to improve production.

In 1942 Franz von Korab, deputy head of the *Abwehr* (German military intelligence service) in Krakow, introduced Schindler to Dr Rudolf Sedlacek a collaborator with the Aid and Rescue Committee. The Committee was based in Budapest and it worked to smuggle

Schindler's desk.

5,000 Polish Jews out of Nazi occupied Europe before the Wehrmacht occupied Hungary in March 1944.

Schindler became the contact between the Committee, the ghetto and Plaszow camp. The Committee gave him money to help the Jews and he also delivered letters and parcels. It also asked him to locate senior Jewish leaders who were in hiding or in Plaszow. He used bribes to move fifteen of them into his factory.

Schindler took many chances in his dealing with Jewish organizations and used his charm and chequebook to stop people delving into his business too deeply. However, people still denounced him and the Gestapo arrested him on three occasions.

Relocating the Factory
Schindler had prepared a register of workers as early as 18 April 1944. The Soviet advances into southern Poland in the summer of 1944 forced the Inspectorate of Concentration Camps to reconsider deploying its workforce. When Göth told him Plaszow was going to be closed down, Schindler decided to relocate to Brünnlitz, near Zwittau, his hometown in the Sudetenland, to avoid his workforce being deported. Schindler also agreed to take sixty workers from Julius Madritsch's sewing factory which had been based in Plaszow since 14 September 1943.

Madritsch had used his factory's profits to buy extra food for his 800 workers. He had employed many families in the factory and made sure their children were placed with Polish families before the ghetto closed. Then when the SS wanted to close down in Plaszow he moved as many workers as possible first to Bochnia and Tarnów ghettos and then to another Silesian labour camp.

Even after paying a large bribe, the Concentration Camp Inspectorate would only allow Schindler to take just over half of his workforce, whose names were on a revised list. A selection was held at the factory on 7 August 1944 and 700 men and 160 women were marched to Plaszow and loaded into cattle trucks ready for deportation. Schindler saw to it that the trucks were showered with water when he heard they had been left on the railway sidings in the blazing sun.

Schindler's flat near Wawel Castle.

On 15 October 1944 a transport carrying the 700 men of Schindler's workforce left for the Sudetenland and six days later the 300 women joined 1,700 others from Plaszow. Poles would continue to run Emalia until the Red Army arrived in January 1945.

The men were taken straight to the new factory at Brünnlitz but the women were taken to Auschwitz-Birkenau extermination camp. They spent the night in the shower block and then were subjected to a selection by the notorious SS doctor, Josef Mengele. Schindler was being held in prison at the time, probably being questioned in connection with Göth's corruption case, but he tried to save them as soon as he was released a few days later.

One version says he sent his secretary Hilda Albrecht to Birkenau to talk to the concentration camp staff while he bribed the right people to get the women out. A different version says the women were sent to Birkenau because they had to be shaved on route to Brünnlitz and it was the only camp en route with a women's section. Either way, the release of the women from the extermination camp was unprecedented.

Virtually all the workers on Schindler's List were in Brünnlitz by early November. The local people were unhappy about having over 1,000 Jews on their doorstep and complained to the authorities. The factory was made a sub-camp of Gross-Rosen concentration camp and the SS administration again demanded barbed-wire, watchtowers, searchlights and accommodation for forty guards.

It cost Schindler a large part of his fortune to move the 250 wagon loads of machinery and set it up, but the operation was all a sham to fool the authorities – he had no intention of making shells. He planned to buy products from other factories and sell them on his own. The guards were kept happy with alcohol and extra food; parties and gifts would make sure the factory inspectors did not look too closely at his business.

Schindler found a couple of railway wagons full of sixty frozen men abandoned in Zwittau at the end of January. Some were still clinging on to life and he took them to the factory, despite the commandant's protests, where his wife Emilie helped care for them in a makeshift hospital. Rabbi Menashe Levertov was also allowed to bury the dead with the correct religious rites.

Everyone was concerned when Amon Göth visited and spent a week in Schindler's company following his release from prison. Some wondered what deals the two were arranging, but they need not have worried. Göth had just visited to collect his belongings Schindler had been looking after.

The Soviets Get Closer

Everyone worried what the guards would do when the Red Army arrived. The commandant, *Obersturmführer* Josef Leipold, was given an order to carry out a selection and send those fit for work to Germany. The rest had to be resettled; in other words murdered.

After Leipold had prisoners dig mass graves in the woods, Schindler saw to it that he was replaced with an elderly reserve officer who preferred an easy life and bribes. But Schindler was taking no chances and he purchased weapons and grenades, telling the new commandant they would be used to defend the camp from marauding Soviet troops.

The Third Reich surrendered to the Allies on 8 May 1945 and while it was a joyous day for many across Europe, it was not a good day for Schindler. The Red Army soldiers would see him as a member of the Nazi Party and a munitions factory owner working for the Wehrmacht. After making his final arrangements and wishing the assembled workforce good luck, he personally thanked several people and gave Abraham Bankier the keys to the factory. A delegation of inmates had packed an escape kit in his car and they gave him a ring engraved with the words *"He who saves a life, saves the world entire,"* a quote from the Talmud.

At midnight he said his final goodbyes in his mechanic's disguise and the workers gave him a letter explaining his deeds, in case he was captured:

> *"We, the undersigned Jews from Krakow, inmates of Plaszow concentration camp, have, since 1940, worked in Director Schindler's business... During the entire period in*

which we worked for Director Schindler he did everything possible to save the lives of the greatest possible number of Jews, in spite of the tremendous difficulties... Director Schindler took care of our sustenance, and as a result, during the whole period of our employment by him and stay at the sub-camp on Lipowa, the Emalia, there was not a single case of unnatural death... Here we are, a gathering of 1,100 people, 800 men and 300 women. All Jewish workers that were inmates in the Plaszow, Gross-Rosen and Auschwitz concentration camps respectively declare wholeheartedly their gratitude towards Director Schindler, and we herewith state that it is exclusively due to his efforts that we were permitted to witness this moment, the end of the war."

After an emotional parting, Schindler his wife and a handful of associates drove off, facing an uncertain future.

The following day a single Soviet soldier arrived at the camp and announced it had been liberated by the Red Army. A total of 1,096 of Schindler's Jews had survived. After murdering Willi, the cruellest kapo, they waited several weeks before leaving the relative safety of the factory. But there were still dangers to avoid as they headed to Krakow. The countryside was filled with marauding Red Army soldiers looking to rob and rape. Only when they made it home did it become clear that they had lost most, if not all, of their families and friends in the Holocaust.

After the War

The Schindlers were virtually destitute because Oskar had spent his fortune keeping the factory open with bribes and black market supplies. They spent four years in Germany before moving to Argentina with a donation from the American Jewish Joint Distribution Committee. There they set up a chicken and coypu farm, but it failed and they returned to Germany and lived separately while Oskar tried to make several businesses work. Former Jewish workers sent donations to the pair and Leopold Page (known as Leopold

Pfefferberg in Poland) set up the Oskar Schindler Survivors Fund in Los Angeles in the 1960s.

Oskar went to Israel in May 1962 and planted a tree in the Yad Vashem garden in Jerusalem. He was recognized as one of the '*Righteous among the Nations*' the following year for saving the lives of 1,200 Jews (Madritsch was honoured the same in 1964). Schindler died in Germany on 9 October 1974, aged 66, and was buried in the Christian cemetery in Jerusalem; the only member of the Nazi Party to be honoured there. Emilie died in 2001, aged 94.

Chapter 10

Plaszow Concentration Camp

In July 1942 SS and Police Leader Julian Scherner gave instructions to open three Jewish labour camps in the Krakow area. Jewish Labour Camp I (*Judenarbeitslager, Julag I*) would be built in the Plaszow district, one mile south of the ghetto, on the site of two Jewish cemeteries on Abrahama St and Jerozolimska St; Julag II and III were in the Bieżanów-Prokocim district, three miles to the south-east.

Building the Camp

The original Julag I site covered fifteen hectares and was situated in a small valley, hidden from the outside world, close to Plaszow railway station. *SS-Unterscharführer* Horst Pilarzik was the first commandant and the construction work was supervised by architect Rudolf Lukas. He appointed five Jewish engineers, Zygmunt Grünberg, Jakub Stendig, Henryk Haber, Berger and Zimmet, to oversee the works; the German Housing and Community Association hired local tradesmen to do the technical work and the Jews did the labouring.

Prisoners walked the mile to and from the ghetto. The women moved earth around in wheelbarrows while the men dug up and laid gravestones to form the main street and the office entrance; the best stones were sold for profit. Privileged prisoners, known as kapos, supervised each group, beating the workers to make them work harder, and the guards sometimes flogged and occasionally shot the prisoners.

A headquarters and guard barracks were built near the entrance while nearby houses were converted for senior staff to live in. Once the site was levelled, Pilarzik formed Barrack Construction units (*Baracken Bau*) of between twenty-five and fifty prisoners and work began on barrack blocks and workshops. Around 1,500 inmates moved into Forced Labour Camp Plaszow (*Zwangsarbeitslager Plaszow*) in November 1942.

Although SS-Oberscharführer Franz Müller ran the camp over the winter, it is *SS-Untersturmführer* Amon Göth who is remembered as Plaszow's commandant. He arrived in February 1943 and the beatings and executions increased. The rate of construction also intensified and 88 barrack blocks were ready in time for the liquidation of the ghetto on 13 and 14 March 1943.

Commandant Amon Göth.

The men were separated from women and children, their luggage was confiscated and valuables and money were surrendered under death threats. Around 4,000, the elderly, the sick and the children,

Moving rocks from the quarry.

were shot behind the quarantine huts while 8,000 were crammed into the barracks even though they were only designed for 4,000.

On 27 March the Ukrainian guards surrounded the barracks and everyone was lined up. It was made clear that anyone found in possession of jewels would be executed and they were given the opportunity to hand over anything valuable hidden about their person. The German guards then began searching them. It was a brutal reminder that life in Plaszow camp was going to be far harder and more dangerous than it had been in the ghetto.

The Camp Layout

Plaszow camp eventually grew into a huge complex with barracks, offices, workshops and facilities, and it covered sixty-four hectares. The staff lived and worked on the east side, either side of Jerozolimska. The north-west side of the camp was split into three with male and female living sections and the kitchen and toilet area; it also had a large parade ground for roll calls. The south-west side of the camp was filled with workshops.

The complex was surrounded with two miles of double electrified barbed-wire fence, each 2.5 metres high; more fences divided the camp into male, female, administration and working sections. There were twelve two-storey watchtowers and the German and Ukrainian guards were armed with machine guns and searchlights. A report leader (*rapportführer*) checked the working parties as they marched through the main gate. The Gestapo used the adjacent Grey House with its interrogation rooms and cells. Across the road was a large guard house with a four-storey watchtower and barracks. *Untersturmführer* Heinrich Balb held property robbed from the Jews in nearby storehouses.

Poles were forced out of the houses along Heltmana (renamed *SS-Strasse*), south of the main gate and they were decorated and improved ready for the camp's senior officers. The motor workshops, kennels and stables were in the south-east corner of the camp, along with two sheds filled with religious items and books stolen from the city's synagogues.

The main road, Hill Street (*Bergenstrasse*), ran west-east

A map of Plaszow concentration camp.

through the camp and divided the barracks from the workshops. The men's barracks were first to the right (north) of the road, surrounding the parade ground. New arrivals were held in the collection camp (*Auffangslager*) behind the men's barracks.

The worst jobs were in the Liban quarry north of the men's camp. Men had to break rocks and load them onto wagons while women hauled them up the ramp out of the quarry. The best jobs were in the bakery, the kitchen, a cold store, a meat processing plant and storehouses, west of the men's camp, in front of the women's barracks.

The slope and high ground to the left (south) of the road was the area called the New Land and it was filled with workshops divided into compounds, many of them owned by the German Equipment Works (Deutsche Ausrüstungswerke, DAW). Blacksmiths, metal smiths, carpenters, electricians, cobblers, clock makers and brush makers worked in over half a dozen large huts closest to the road. Then came three construction offices next to the print shop where secret documents were sometimes reproduced at night; inmates were shot after completing the sensitive work. Finally, there were twenty barracks lining Industry Street on the south side of the camp, and they were filled with tailors, seamstresses, furriers and upholsterers.

In the autumn of 1943 work started on improving the camp's security and infrastructure. The site grew to eighty hectares in area as the number of barrack blocks and workshops increased to 200. The number of inmates was increased to 25,000 and the camp's contribution to the war effort increased accordingly.

Villas for senior officers and executives of the munitions company were renovated and extended. A new headquarters building, a hospital and a new parade ground were built for the guards. A clothing store, showers, delousing block and a quarantine facility were added for the prisoners. A railway siding meant prisoners and stores could be brought right to the camp gates while a crematorium disposed of bodies. Fire was a concern and some barracks were moved to increase the gaps between them; water ponds were also dug for the camp's fire brigade.

Camp Life

Around 300 prisoners were crammed into every wooden barrack block, each measuring 40 metres long and 10 metres wide; they had no lights and little ventilation. They had to sleep on the three storey wooden bunk beds, without mattresses or blankets, and huddled together under their coats for warmth. The washhouse was a single

Workshops at the front while barracks surround the parade ground.

trough where up to 400 people pushed and shoved as they splashed water on their faces. The toilet block had a wide plank and up to seventy prisoners at a time had to balance over an open cesspit while queues of waiting people urged them to hurry up.

SS-Rottenführer Wilhelm Kunde and a German Jew named Meyer ran the kitchens and they often spent part of their budget on providing better meals for the camp guards, in the hope of earning the commandant's approval. The prisoners' diet consisted of poor quality coffee and a piece of bread for breakfast, thin vegetable soup for lunch and coffee in the evening. The Jewish Order Service ran the bakery and camp kitchen until early 1944 and it eventually had sixty 80-gallon soup cauldrons.

While Fischer, the kitchen deputy, tried to stop the guards stealing food, the soup was often made from leftovers and scraps from the German kitchens. Although some tried to smuggle items in, it was both risky and expensive. Göth was open to bribery and he allowed Julius Madritsch to give his tailors and seamstresses extra bread in return for money.

Plaszow camp did not have any showers until May 1944 and each barrack block took it in turn to shower. Once a month the 300 prisoners had to undress and cram into the block hoping to get wet under one of the shower heads. Their clothes were disinfected in the nearby fumigation block, but the cleansing operation was not for the prisoners comfort, it was to stop typhoid outbreaks.

Punishment

Life was cruel in the camp and the prisoners were subjected to regular insults, humiliation and beatings. The work was hard, the rules were many and so were the punishments, particularly for anyone caught loitering or working slowly. Prisoners were not allowed to look at the guards and they had to take off their cap and continue walking at a fast past when they passed one. The leader of a group of prisoners had to shout out the order *'mützen ab'* (caps off), and everyone had to look down if a guard approached. The order *'mützen auf'* (caps on) was given when he moved on and work resumed.

Many of the guards had dogs and they used them to intimidate and sometimes bite the prisoners. Göth's favourite was a particularly vicious hound called Rolf and the prisoners had to call it *Herr Hund*. He would enjoy watching it maul a prisoner and would then shoot the victim.

There were punishments for any small offence and floggings were often held in front of the rest of the prisoners. Offenders were usually given 25 or 50 lashes and they had to count them out loud, thanking the officer at the end. Anyone who fainted was revived and the beating started all over again. Serious infractions resulted in a spell in a standing cell, a tiny room with few air holes and no room to sit or crouch. Another punishment for a serious crime was a posting to the penal company in the nearby quarry and work from 4am to 10pm on half rations. The company kapo, Ivan, hassled and beat the prisoners while the quarry supervisor, a German called Lehmer, shot those who could not keep up.

There were a few escape attempts but the consequences were harsh – ten or twenty people from the escapees hut or work party would be executed. It was the same if anyone was caught smuggling.

The Commandant's House.

After the initial shootings near the entrance, regular mass executions, including 400 people shot on 19 September 1943, were carried out in a nineteenth century artillery earthworks on the south-west side of the camp. It was called *Hujowa Gorka* (or *H-Gorka*) after SS-Unterscharführer Albert Hujar (the Poles called it Huj Hill; Prick Hill). More executions were carried out in another artillery fortification on the south side of the camp called *Cipowy Dolek* (*C-Dolek*).

The Camp Hospital

A hospital was set up in three barracks on the west side of the camp. Each block had forty-five beds and there was a shower, and delousing and toilet facilities. Doctor Leon Gross was chosen to be the chief medical officer because he was a young, inexperienced man who followed orders. While he cared little for the patients, the forty nurses from the ghetto hospital did what they could to comfort them.

The hospital was soon overcrowded, with up to three patients squeezed onto each bed. They were left unwashed, hungry and without visitors. It was short of everything and the Jewish Aid Agency did what it could to acquire medicines, dressings and money for extra food and forwarded them to the Central Welfare Council for distribution.

A young German dentist, *SS-Obersturmführer* Wilhelm Jäger, was appointed chief medical officer and *SS-Oberscharführer* Walter Schwank his deputy when the camp was taken over by the SS. Jäger also cared little for his patients, murdering many with petrol injections.

In spring of 1944 the Institute of German Work in the East set up a blood transfusion unit in the hospital. The staff forcibly took blood from young female prisoners and sent it to hospitals treating German soldiers.

Polish Prisoners

Starting in July 1943, Poles were sent to Plaszow for punishment for breaking one or more of the many General Government's laws; this was known as 're-education'. Around 1,500 prisoners were soon being held for short periods for *"...additional training in civic virtues for a variety of felonies"*. They were later held close to the camp's guardhouse in similar unpleasant conditions to the Jews. The Poles' commandant was the sadistic *SS-Untersturmführer* Lorenz Landsdorfer who was nicknamed the 'Hawk' or the 'Messenger of Death' (*Meshullah*).

Dr Ludwik Zurowski collected food, mail and medicines across the city and had it smuggled in so the sub-camp doctor Wladyslaw Sztencel could distribute it amongst the prisoners. Sztencel was soon caught, executed and replaced by Doctor Stanislaw Jagielski. In December 1943 the Central Welfare Council began delivering food parcels made by relatives but the SS men stole anything of value and the prisoners remained hungry.

The Polish sector was merged with the rest of the camp when the SS took over the camp in January 1944. They were subject to the same abuses and punishments as the Jews. The fit were often sent to work in Germany, the sick were taken to Auschwitz-Birkenau. Prisoners from Montelupich and other prisons were often brought to Plaszow to be shot.

Concentration Camp

In January 1944 the SS took over Plaszow and it was renamed Concentration Camp Plaszow at Krakow (*Konzentrationslager Plaszow bei Krakau*). Göth was promoted to *SS-Hauptsturmführer* and given a new title, '*der Kommandeur*', and *Oberscharführer* Lorenz Landsdorfer was appointed camp commander, responsible for the day-to-day running of the camp. The Jewish OD police were demoted to run the barrack blocks and one hundred SS guards took over, their work made easier due the electrification of the perimeter.

Amon Göth shooting at prisoners from his balcony.

Göth soon discovered that he had to reduce his black market activities now he was working for the SS. His staff had to follow directives from the Concentration Camp Inspectorate and both record and justify activities. The guards also had to limit their brutality, or at least be more subtle in how they acted. They were supposed to justify and record punishment but few did, they simply falsified the records. Unlawful beatings were supposed to stop and floggings were reduced to twenty-five lashes but the rules were often ignored and the paperwork forgotten. Göth still strutted around the camp, randomly murdering people for no reason and he also considered it 'sport' to shoot inmates from his villa balcony, some 300 metres from the parade ground.

The conversion of the camp meant that Jews from other areas were deported to Plaszow to work and Krakow's Jews were eager for news. Unfortunately, the first group were full of stories of mass executions and death camps, confirming rumours that had so far been dismissed.

An Uprising
Despite the difficulties and risks, a small group of prisoners planned to hold an armed uprising. By February 1944 six groups of ten had formed and they were kept informed of events in the outside world by a radio hidden in the clockmaker's workshop. They made duplicate keys, stole two pistols and ammunition and made a stash of home-made grenades.

Göth's maid, Helena Sternlicht copied relevant German documents but Adam Sztab's false pass did not fool the Ukrainian guarding the armoury. Göth badly beat Sztab and hanged him in the barrack square with a placard around his neck stating, 'Anyone concealing a weapon will die like this'. The uprising went no further.

Selections
Hitler organized Operation Margarethe, a plan to seize Hungary's vital facilities, when he heard Hungarian Prime Minister Miklós Kállay was discussing an armistice with the Allies, with Regent Miklós Horthy's approval. The Wehrmacht occupied Hungary on 19

March 1944 and the SS immediately began deporting Hungarian Jews to Auschwitz-Birkenau. Those fit for work were sent on to labour camps while the rest were murdered in the gas chambers.

SS-Standartenführer Gerhard Maurer, deputy Inspector of Concentration Camps, asked Amon Göth to accept 10,000 fit Jews and told him to send 1,500 inmates to Birkenau to make space for them. On the morning of 7 May 1944 plans were put in place to conduct a health inspection under the motto 'proper work for everyone'. Guards surrounded the parade ground during the morning roll call and two tables were set up, covered in prisoner files.

All the prisoners were made to strip and stand in front of *SS-Hauptsturmführer* Dr Maximilian Blancke as he inspected their physical condition, a humiliating experience. *SS-Hauptscharführer* Landsdorfer and OD-man Marcel Goldberg listed the elderly, the sick, the disabled and children under fourteen; they wrote down 1,400 names.

Guards parade ready for a selection.

A week later the process was repeated, only this time it was used as a distraction. A few weeks earlier 286 children had been moved into Szymon Koch's kindergarten barracks. While parents were allowed a daily visit, many chose to smuggle their children back into their barracks, hiding them in all kinds of unpleasant places while they were at work.

The selection was used as a cover while the children were being loaded onto lorries. Cheerful music blaring from the loudspeakers drowned out the screams when the parents saw the lorries driving away and the guards had to fight to hold them back. Göth announced they were being taken to basketwork classes but he was lying. They were taken to Birkenau and gassed.

A few days later the Hungarians began arriving, followed by Slovakian Jews and others from labour camps which were closing. Plaszow could not cope and Göth was allowed to send 6,000 Hungarian women to Auschwitz-Birkenau and another 5,000 in August. Transports also located many Jewish prisoners to labour camps across the Reich in the summer of 1944.

Closing the Camp

Kommandeur Amon Göth was arrested on 13 September 1944, not for the murder of hundreds of Jews, but for stealing and selling their confiscated possessions which had belonged to the Reich. The replacement commandant, *SS-Obersturmführer* Arnold Büscher, had orders to remove all evidence of the heinous crimes committed at Plaszow, deport the prisoners and close the camp.

The first job was to get rid of the mass graves around the camp and a kommando (numbering 80 increasing to 180) spent a month exhuming the hundreds of corpses. They were burnt on pyres, casting a sickly smell over the area, and the prisoners spread the ash around the camp.

On 15 October 4,500 men were deported in cattle wagons to Gross-Rosen concentration camp, 150 miles to the north-west. A few days after, 1,000 women were transported to Auschwitz-Birkenau, forty miles to the west. Few would survive longer than a few weeks; some were murdered straight away. Some of the Poles were sent to work in Germany, others dug anti-tank ditches and the rest were sent to Gross-Rosen concentration camp.

By the end of the month forty guards supervised 600 Jews and handful of Poles as they dismantled barracks and loaded them onto trains so they could be re-used. The cadre of camp staff sent the important files and documents to Berlin and burnt the rest. The last group of prisoners to reach the camp were thirty inmates from Montelupich jail on 28 November. Half were executed immediately and the rest joined in the clearing work.

After the War

Plaszow camp finally closed on 15 January 1945 as Red Army troops approached Krakow. Most of the prisoners had already been deported but *SS-Oberscharführer* Kurt Schupke marched the final group of 600 west, heading for Auschwitz. A few hid in the ruins of the deserted camp and waited for the Soviets to arrive.

It is believed nearly 100,000 men, women and children could have spent time inside Plaszow camp during its two-and-a-half year existence. Around 10,000 people are estimated to have been murdered and buried in the area. The destruction of the camp records means that the exact figure will never be known.

Chapter 11

The Misery Continues

Katyn Wood Massacre

On 13 April 1943 Berlin announced that mass graves of Polish officers had been discovered in Katyn Wood, near Smolensk, and that they had been shot by Red Army troops. Two days later Moscow angrily declared they had been executed by the Wehrmacht. General Wladyslaw Sikorski, Prime Minister of the Polish Government in Exile, asked the International Red Cross to investigate and Berlin did the same. The Soviet Union then broke diplomatic relations with the Polish government, on the grounds it was collaborating with Nazi Germany.

International forensic experts and criminologists arrived and began digging at Katyn on 28 April. They took the remains to the National Forensic Institute in Krakow where Doctor Ian Robel supervised the investigation. The *Krakow Messenger* published photographs of the graves a couple of weeks later and the people of Poland were horrified to see the names of the 4,500 executed officers.

The authorities continued to use Katyn in anti-Soviet propaganda until the Poles believed it was the Soviets. It was 1990 before the Russian authorities admitted the Secret Police (NKVD) had murdered 22,000 officers, half the Polish officer corps, in the Second World War, including those buried at Katyn.

A Different Approach

As the tide of the war turned against Germany some senior Nazis talked about softening their views against the Poles. The Battle of Stalingrad came to an end with a Red Army victory in February 1943

Public executions became more commonplace.

and Hans Frank stated that *"revolvers, bullets and concentration camps* [had] *proven pointless"*. In June both Frank and Krakow District Governor, Ludwig Losacker, asked Hitler for a more lenient approach against the Poles in the General Government. Frank followed it up on 23 July by telling the Central Welfare Council representatives he wanted to improve cooperation with them. Five days later the Wola Justowska district, west of the city centre, was searched, twenty citizens were murdered and another eighty were deported to Auschwitz.

As Frank continued to talk about a 'soft line' against the Poles, the message could have only been a ruse to get their cooperation because the executions continued. Over 330 people were murdered in just three days late in October; some shot in secret and others hung in public. Meanwhile, Frank showed his true colours when he had

Governor Dr Ludwig Losacker arrested and sentenced to death for his lenient treatment of the Poles and the Jews. The sentence was commuted and he was conscripted into the SS with the rank of private.

The Summer of 1944

There were momentous events across Europe in the summer of 1944. The Allies broke the German Gustav Line on the Italian Front in May, after six months of bitter fighting. Allied troops landed in Normandy on the north coast of France on 6 June, at the start of Operation Overlord, creating the long awaited second front.

On 22 June the Red Army launched Operation Bagration on the Eastern Front, smashing through Army Group Centre and across the Polish border. The Wehrmacht would suffer over 550,000 casualties and lose more than 2,000 tanks and 57,000 vehicles in a few weeks. Then a month later the Lvov-Sandomierz Offensive was launched through southern Poland and Ukraine, heading straight for Krakow.

On 20 July 1944 there was the very nearly successful assassination attempt on Adolf Hitler, codename Valkyrie, at his Wolf's Lair headquarters in northern Poland. The crumbling of the German fronts undermined its allies' confidence and both Hungary and Slovakia were hit by uprisings in August while Romania switched to the Allied side. The following month both Bulgaria and Finland changed sides.

While German propaganda suppressed news of Allied successes in Krakow it could not hide the fact that the Wehrmacht was falling back in disorder. The Red Army breakthrough caused a panic evacuation of eastern Lower Poland by the German military. The sight of soldiers selling arms, ammunition and equipment from their camps in the park around the old city walls brought criminals and underground members flocking to the area. Soldiers were also buying everything they could, driving up prices and increasing black market activities.

The people of Krakow watched with growing nervousness as the Germans pulled out, taking everything they could from Polish and Jewish businesses on their way. Officials rushed around, packing up their offices and apartments, burning any documents they could not take with them.

Krakow was a central rallying point for German officials and the while General Government did what it could to control their evacuation, Polish underground's Bureau of Information and Propaganda increased the chaos by sending out bogus summonses to German families. The Royal Castle and the National Museum were prepared for evacuation, libraries and museums were emptied and military hospitals were reduced in size. Steps were also taken to deport prisoners from Krakow's prisons and camps.

Although the military news from the Eastern Front was good, the political news was not. A Polish Committee of National Liberation had been formed in Moscow under Soviet control and it was refusing to recognize the Polish Government in Exile. It began running Soviet-occupied territories from its headquarters in Lublin and even handed over a huge area of Polish territory to the Soviet Union.

The Warsaw Uprising

On 1 August 1944 the Home Army rose up in Warsaw as part of Operation Tempest and the people of Krakow welcomed the news. Five days later Krakow's Higher SS and Police Leader, *SS-Obergruppenführer* Wilhelm Koppe, appealed for men to dig air raid trenches in a ruse to stop an uprising in the city. Few turned up, giving him the excuse to carry out mass arrests. The Secret Police knocked on doors while the German and Polish police rounded up all the young men they found on the streets.

On 6 August over 6,000 young men were arrested and taken to Plaszow camp while many others went into hiding or joined the underground on what became known as 'Black Sunday'. The Central Welfare Office was closed for a while, so parcels could not be sent to Polish prisoners and the department dealing with Auschwitz was permanently shut. The *Aktion* brought the city to a standstill and those needed to get the city moving were released at once. But two days later the Czarodziejska district, on the south bank of the Vistula, was raided while another 1,150 people were rounded up during the last week of August.

On 8 September the people of Krakow noticed a nauseous smell and occasional flurries of ash in the air. It came from the direction of Plaszow. It lasted for nearly six weeks, and few knew it came from huge funeral pyres as every last corpse was dug up and burnt as the camp closed.

By the time the Warsaw uprising came to an end on 2 October 1944, thousands of refugees had left the city and around 15,000 descended on Krakow, looking for a place to stay in the overcrowded city. The Central Welfare Office and Polish Welfare Committee could not cope and appeals to the International Red Cross in Switzerland resulted in a train load of food reaching the city in mid-October; more would arrive over the winter. Archbishop Sapieha appealed for help and monks and nuns set up shelters and soup kitchens in monasteries and convents. Others held collections and charity events but the people of Krakow had little to give, causing some resentment. The Polish Underground State moved to Krakow after Warsaw fell and while it gave money to help the refugees, there was never enough to go round.

Preparing to Defend the City

General Heinz Guderian, the Chief of Staff of the Army's High Command (*Oberkommando des Heeres*, OKH) had wanted to build an East Wall (*Ostwall*) to stop the next Red Army offensive. Krakow was on the route to the important industrial region in Upper Silesia and the authorities appealed for help building fortifications to protect the city in August 1944; the appeals were ignored. Propaganda was then issued about the savagery of the Red Army soldiers to scare people into volunteering. That too failed and people were rounded up.

The forced labourers prepared field defences and improved existing fortifications to the late nineteenth century forts on the east side of the city. While they dug trenches, excavated tank traps and built barriers, army engineers fortified buildings, built strongpoints and laid mines. Even parks and other open spaces were converted ready to be used as runways.

A poster calling for Poles to help stop the Bolshevik hordes.

The Final Winter

The final winter of the war was a difficult time. No one dared go out at night because of the strict curfew and only muggers roamed the dark streets. In November 1944 the authorities took advantage of the miserable conditions by putting up posters, encouraging Polish men to join one of the Wehrmacht's auxiliary services. Although a wage, food and accommodation were offered, only 321 men enlisted.

The number of round-ups and executions increased, and it became harder to acquire fuel and food. The authorities also shut down many factories and the Polish workers were forced to help those digging trenches in the rain and snow.

The Wehrmacht had been forced to move its troops from Krakow to hold the front line along the Vistula, only 100 miles east of the city. It left a void in law and order and the Home Army stepped up its campaign to kill informers and collaborators.

Hans Frank vowed to help the police restore control on 12 December 1944 and hundreds of Germans were enlisted into paramilitary formations, so they could stamp out criminal activities. More roundups were made and the homeless exiles from Warsaw were particularly vulnerable. Over 1,700 were held as forced labourers on 6 and 7 January alone.

Although it was dangerous to talk about the Soviet Union's progress in public, everyone spoke about it in private, worried what new terrors the Red Army soldiers would bring. Rumours that German engineers were preparing buildings for demolition and building fortifications was an added concern. One of the few places people could gather was in church; churches were full of those seeking company and solace in difficult times.

Further humiliations occurred in the run-up to Christmas when the Special Service searched shops for contraband on 18 and 24 December. Goods worth 30 million zloty were confiscated and around 250 shop owners spent Christmas in prison under false charges of selling illegal items. The searches had been nothing more than a government sponsored robbery.

Chapter 12

The End of the War

By the start of January 1945 the end was close for General Government's headquarters. The Red Army was poised to advance astride the River Vistula, straight through Krakow and into the Silesian industrial area beyond.

The Red Army Approaches

The battle plan was for Marshal Ivan Konev's First Ukrainian Front to exploit its bridgehead over the Vistula and advance north of Krakow while General Ivan Petrov's Fourth Ukrainian Front moved along the south bank, towards the east side of the city. They both faced General Friedrich Schultz's Seventeenth Army.

The main forces concentrated east of Tarnow, fifty miles east of Krakow, while two bogus armoured corps equipped with 4,000 dummy tanks and 1,000 imitation assault guns assembled to the north around Debica. Although Seventeenth Army learnt all about the fake force, it was still in a precarious position astride the Vistula.

First Ukrainian Front attacked from the Sandomierz bridgehead on 12 January 1945, making use of its sixteen-to-one advantage in tanks, and advanced along the north bank of the Vistula, behind Seventeenth Army's left flank. The General Government went into evacuation mode as institutions were instructed to evacuate within forty-eight hours. All Polish men and women were ordered to report to their Labour Office, ready to be transported to Germany, but everyone stayed away, even though they could hear the sound of battle in the distance.

The final winter and the end is in sight.

German Evacuation

As the Fifteenth Ukrainian Front advanced towards Krakow, 60th Army faced heavy resistance fighting through the fortifications protecting the city. To the south, 38th Army also moved slowly through difficult terrain. The breakthrough came on the night of 13 January when 59th Army reached Miechow, twenty-five miles north of the city.

The General Government held their last meeting on the 15th. In one last act of cruelty, there was a final mass execution on the same day in the Dabie district, on the east side of the city. At 2pm on the 17th Hans Frank and his entourage left the city followed by the General Government's staff and their families. Offices were cleared, apartments were abandoned and shops were plundered. The following day the Gestapo set fire to Silesia House and left the city.

The Assault on Krakow

On 18 January Marshal Konev joined General Ivan Korovnikov, at 59th Army headquarters in Skala, fifteen miles north of Krakow. Infantry were soon advancing slowly through the north and east suburbs towards the city centre. Although 12th Armoured Brigade encountered tank traps and minefields immediately west of the city, 13th Armoured Brigade cleared the Zwierzyniec district and its tanks reached the north bank of the Vistula by mid-afternoon. They then turned towards the city centre, only to be stopped along Straszewskiego, 300 metres from the Main Market Square. It meant the German escape route west was cut.

But the breakthrough came from the north-west when General Korovnikov reinforced General Pavel Poluboyarov's IV Armoured Corps in its battle in the Krowodrza district. The huge JS-2 tanks of 29th Heavy Tank Regiment proved too much for the German armour and they reached the Market Square by the mid-afternoon.

As Soviet troops worked their way into the city centre, Jozef Hryniewiecki and Wladyslaw Rajpold entered the Royal Castle. They climbed the Senatorial Tower, hoisted the Polish national flag and sang the national anthem. No one noticed the flag only half way up the pole and upside down; all that mattered was it symbolized the end of the German occupation.

Red Army troops along the Vistula.

General Wilhelm Koppe was in command of the armed forces in Krakow but all he could do was try and stop the withdrawal turning into a rout. Army Group B wanted Seventeenth Army to protect Upper Silesia's industrial region so General Josef Harpe ordered General Friedrich Schultz to evacuate the city. The city streets were jammed with civilian and military vehicles overloaded with people in the frantic dash over the Vistula bridges ahead of the Red Army troops.

After fierce fighting at the bridgeheads, the engineers blew the three bridges at dusk before the Soviets could capture them, leaving the rest to walk across the iced-over river. By dawn the city centre was clear; after five years, four months and twelve days the German occupation had ended.

The battle east of the city lasted a few more days as 60th Army and 38th Army fought their way through the city suburbs but the rearguards were eventually overcome as the Germans withdrew. By 23 January the locals were relieved to learn the front line was moving west.

The Red Army had captured Krakow for the cost of 1,900 casualties. The number of German losses are unknown but civilian casualties had been low due to the encirclement manoeuvre and the chaotic evacuation. Krakow's historic centre had been saved from destruction and a massive 324-gun salute in Moscow celebrated the news.

The Soviets Arrive

The Germans had taken all the lorries, carts and horses they could find in their rush to leave Krakow. They had also removed a lot of parts and spares from the utilities and damaged the tram depots, while the lack of power meant services were disrupted for a few days. The demolition of the Vistula bridges damaged the riverside gasworks in the Kazimierz district, causing blackouts for two days. The Germans had also cut off the water supply and set fire to warehouses filled with food and other essential supplies and the people of Krakow turned out in force, in the hope of rescuing something before it all went up in flames.

The Germans had gone, the city had not been razed to the ground but the local residents had little to celebrate. The Red Army soldiers robbed food stores, stole goods and requisitioned apartments. They also requisitioned thirty-five tons of meat left in the city abattoir by the Wehrmacht. The people of Krakow were going to have to go hungry for a little while longer. But there was worse to come as men were deported to labour camps in the Soviet Union and women were raped.

Those who had been released from labour camps across Europe also faced robbery, abuse and assaults as they made their difficult journey home. Many decided to stay in displaced persons camps (DP camps) in Germany, Austria and Italy rather than head into Soviet occupied territory. Those who risked the trek then faced the shock of finding people living in their homes, their things sold and their friends and family gone; many of them dead.

A City Saved

Communist propaganda created a myth around the liberation of

Krakow after the war. The story centred on Marshal Konev's 'manoeuvre that saved the city'. It played on the fact that his troops had bypassed the north side of the city and forced the Germans to make a run for it across the Vistula.

The propaganda stated that Konev had been instructed not to fire his artillery at the city. It also explained how the Soviet intelligence services and Polish Communists had discovered the Germans had mined parts of the city and linked all the mines to a central detonation point in a fort in the Pasternik district. Red Army troops had seized the fort before the German engineers detonated the explosives, saving many historic buildings.

Newspapers and radio remembered the events every year after the war; a book was published and a film made. But a study of military documents after the fall of the Soviet Union in 1991 revealed that there had been no such order cancelling artillery fire and that there had been no central detonation point. Krakow had been saved from destruction because the Germans had abandoned the city.

The Home Army Disbands

But what of the Home Army during the liberation of the city? The Red Army advance in the summer of 1944 had left the east half of the Home Army's Krakow Region under Soviet control. Colonel Przemyslaw Nakoniecznikoff-Klukowski (codename Crow II) soon heard worrying reports about Soviet crack-downs on the Polish underground with members being arrested, deported and executed. The Home Army had exposed itself fighting the Germans and the organization could not go back underground because it was too big and well-known.

Commanders of the Polish Underground State spent the winter planning how to transfer the Home Army members to a new organization, codenamed Independence (or NIE which is also Polish for 'no'). The Soviet offensive on 12 January 1945 prompted the announcement of plans at a meeting on 16 January 1945 in Krakow. Two days later Colonel Nakoniecznikoff-Klukowski issued a farewell order to the soldiers of Krakow and the city's Home Army disbanded the following day.

A few groups of Home Army soldiers went onto Krakow's streets to protect public buildings from the Germans but they chose not to help the Red Army troops as they fought their way through the city, having heard how their comrades further east had been treated by the NKVD.

The Regional Delegation stayed hidden and stopped work but it did not take long for the NKVD to track down the leaders. On 27 March the leaders of the Polish Underground State were captured and deported to Moscow for a show trial. Then the NKVD arrested the Krakow Government Delegate, Jan Jakobiec, on 17 April and the Krakow Region Commandant, Colonel Przemyslaw Nakoniecznikoff-Klukowski, three days later. Despite the round-ups and arrests, Colonel Ian Rzepecki established the Armed Forces Delegation for Poland, and underground activities continued; only this time they were against the Soviet administration.

Chapter 13

Visiting Krakow

Krakow is the second largest city in Poland and it is situated in Silesia, in the south-west of the country. John Paul II International Airport is seven miles west of the city; the flight time is two hours from London and a little longer from other UK airports. While flight schedules change every year, there are plenty of routes to the airport, particularly during the summer months, because Krakow is a popular destination in its own right. It is one of the most beautiful cities in Europe and is a popular place to visit for a short city break. You can either take the train, a bus or a taxi from the airport to the city. You can then either take the tram or a taxi to your hotel.

Krakow has a medieval city centre which is surrounded by Communist era buildings. Most of the hotels are within walking distance of the city centre where you will find plenty of restaurants and bars surrounded by elegant buildings. There is lots of choice and something for all tastes in the way of entertainment, food and drink.

Basic English is spoken nearly everywhere and younger people usually have an excellent command of the language. You will find that a few words of Polish raise a smile. But the Polish language is difficult to read and understand and you will have to get used to reading Polish street names if you use a street map to navigate the city.

You can easily walk around the centre of the city and elderly trams run regularly around the perimeter of the old town. You buy your ticket at the stop and validate it by getting it stamped in the machine on board.

The city has the largest medieval market place in Europe, the

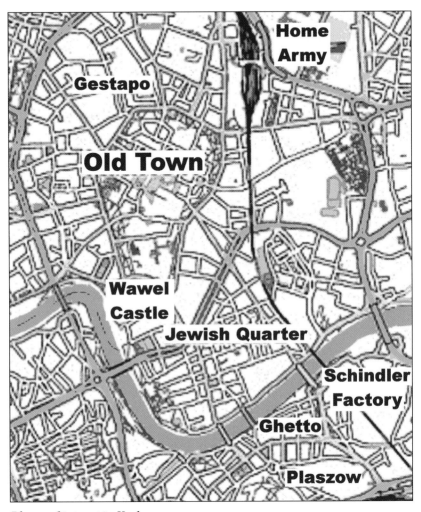

Places of interest in Krakow.

Rynek Glowny, with its huge market hall, clock tower and St Mary's Basilica. The large open space is surrounded by the streets where round-ups were once held and members of the underground once prowled. What follows is a list of the main sights discussed in the book, many of which have museums or memorials related to Second World War events. You need at least three days to visit all the relevant sights, in particular the sites related to Steven Spielberg's 1993 film

Schindler's List. An extra day is needed if you intend to visit the Auschwitz-Birkenau camps which are covered in the companion volume to this, *Auschwitz: The Nazi Solution.* The camps are an hour's drive to the west and there are plenty of coach tours you can book at your hotel or at one of the street agencies. Alternatively you can take a taxi, a relatively inexpensive option (compared to UK taxis), or hire a car.

Wawel Castle
The castle on Wawel Hill is actually a number of structures built around a large courtyard; work started on it in the fourteenth century. It is now the most important historical and cultural centre in Poland. You can visit the State Rooms, the Royal Private Apartments, the Lost Wawel exhibition, the Oriental Art exhibition and the Royal Gardens. There is even a Dragon's Den, once 'home' to the legendary Wawel dragon. It was also home to the Governor-General and the Higher SS and Police Chief.

The individual museums open from 9am until 6pm in the summer and from 9am until 5pm in the winter. Get there early in the day because it does get busy and numbers are limited. To guarantee entry and avoid long queues, you may want to call tel. (+48 12) 422 16 97 to reserve tickets for the exhibition you wish to see in advance. Tickets can be collected at the Wawel visitor centre reservation office at least thirty minutes before the reserved tour time. You can only visit the Royal Apartments with a guide. The general contact details are: (+48 12) 422 5155 ext. 219, e-mail: informacja@wawel.edu.pl.

About 300 metres north of the castle's north gate is where Oskar Schindler finally ended up living. He rented apartment 2 at 7 Straszewskiego, a confiscated Jewish apartment. It is now a private residence.

The Krakow Memory Trail
The city operates a discount ticket for those visiting the three city-run museums; that is the Schindler Factory, the ghetto's Eagle Pharmacy and the Gestapo museum on Pomorska Street. They can be purchased at the Visitor Centre at Sukiennice, Rynek Główny 1

The Market Hall.

(the Cloth Hall, the Market Square, 1), a good place for any advice. The prices are 23 zloty (19 zloty concession) and 55 for a family group. A ticket is valid for seven days from purchase. Online booking is available at Online booking at www.mhk.pl.

The elegant cloth hall is well worth a visit, with its dazzling array of shops. It also houses the National Museum on the first floor.

The People of Krakow in Times of Terror

The museum in the Gestapo headquarters at 2 Pomorska Street, in the north-west suburbs, has two parts. There are a number of cells in the basement where you can see the messages carved in the plaster by the prisoners. The place is claustrophobic and eerie but it brings home the terror of the Gestapo like nothing else. On the floor above is a museum explaining how the Einsatzgruppen brought terror to the city and how the Security Police, the Security Service and the Gestapo worked.

From November to March the museum is open Tuesday, Wednesday and Friday 9am to 4pm; Saturday and Sunday 10am to

5pm and Thursdays 12 noon to 7pm. In the summer it is open Tuesday to Sunday 10am to 5pm. Entrance is 6 zloty (5 zloty concessions) and 12 zloty for a family ticket. Admission is free on Tuesdays. The cells are free to enter if you do not want to go into the main museum. Contact via (+48 12) 6331414, 6311001, 6311002 and e-mail: pomorska@mhk.pl. (Note 0048 is the country code and 12 is the city code).

Podgórze Ghetto and the Eagle Pharmacy
The ghetto was established in the Podgórze district, on the south bank of the Vistula, either five minutes in a taxi (or a 45 minute walk) from the city centre. Alternatively take the tram for Podgórze and get off at Ghetto Heroes Square (*Plac Bohaterow Getta*). The ghetto is quite small (only 500 metres by 400 metres) and it takes less than ten minutes to walk from end to end.

The Eagle Pharmacy.

The apartment blocks are the same as they were in days of the ghetto and the principal buildings have plaques by the door, reminding the visitor what happened there. Although it is an average city district, the history gives it an eerie feel. Visit the Eagle Pharmacy and see the photographs from ghetto years before walking round.

Tadeusz Pankiewicz's pharmacy is at the south end of the square where workers, including Schindler's, assembled before heading off for work. It was also where ID parades were held and people were gathered before they were marched off to the transports. The police station is at the north end of the square and the steel chairs represent the 1,000s of Jews who had to frequently line up here.

The Eagle Pharmacy (*Apteka Pod Orlem*) is now a museum which tells the story of the ghetto and the pharmacy. The museum opens 9am to 5pm Tuesday to Sunday; it is free on Mondays but only open from 10am to 2pm. It closes every second Tuesday of the month. The price is 10 zloty (8 zloty concession) and 20 zloty for a family ticket; extra for an English audio guide.

There were always long queues outside the Labour Office at 10 Jozefinska, as people waited to be allocated work. The ghetto hospice was established in the same building. The hospital was next door and patients were massacred in both buildings when the ghetto was closed in March 1943.

The nearby Judenrat offices at 2 Limanowskiego were a busy place. All sorts of enquiries were dealt with, including apartment allocations and making sure that new decrees were implemented. The only Polish run business in the ghetto was the Optima Factory which made glasses at 9 Wegierska. Young children were taught in secret in the backyard. Patients were also massacred at the infirmary at 15 Limanowskiego. Orphans lived at 31 Jozefinska for a while until the OD police expanded from next door and they were forced to squeeze in with the older children at 31 Jozefinska.

At 27 Lwowska is a short stretch of ghetto wall with its gravestone shaped tops. The plaque reads: "Here they lived, suffered and died at the hands of the German torturers. From here they began their final journey to the death camps." Prisoners were assembled

A remaining section of ghetto wall.

here and marched to Plaszow station, en route to Belzec extermination camp.

The Schindler Factory Museum

The administration building of the Emalia factory has been turned into a museum which covers all aspects of life in wartime Krakow, including the occupation, the ghetto, the Schindler factory and the Plaszow camp. It is at 4 Lipowa street in the industrial district of Zablocie, three kilometres southeast of the old town centre. It is a five minute taxi drive, or there is a tram stop in Plac Bohaterow Getta.

The museum is open Tuesday to Sunday from 10am to 6pm and prices are 15 zloty (concession 13 zloty) and 40 zloty for a family ticket. Guided tours in English for groups of twenty or more are 16 zloty per person and it is extra for an English audio guide. The museum is free (no groups) on Mondays between 10am and 2pm (closed first Monday of every month) but numbers are limited.

Contact on (+48) 122571017, 122570095 or 122570096 and
<u>fabrykaschindlera@mhk.pl</u>.

Plaszow Concentration Camp

The concentration camp is one mile south of Podgórze ghetto, close
to the Plaszow tram stop. There is nothing remaining to remind us
that 1,000s of prisoners were once housed here because the huts and
fences were torn down. But once you get your bearings there are
things to see and the layout comes alive.

The distinctive Grey House (*Szary Dom*) stands alone on the
west side of Jerozolimska. It stood next to the main gate and it was
there that the Gestapo questioned and interrogated people. Heading

The Gestapo's Grey House.

south along Heltmana, the fifth house on the right (west) side is the Red House (*Czerwony Dom*) which was the commandant's villa.

Return to the Grey House and take note of the information board, to get your bearings. Heading west into the camp area you pass Chaim Iakob Abrahamer's grave, the only headstone which remains of the two Jewish cemeteries which were once here. The camp was deliberately built on them and the prisoners' first job was to use the gravestones to make the camp roads.

Continue past the site of the main gate and along the gravel path, up the small valley. We can see the outline of the parade ground has been marked out with gravel to the right (north); we can also see the overgrown fire water ponds. The men's barracks surrounded it while workshops covered the slopes to the left (south). The workshops continued all the way along the left side of what was called Hill Street (*Bergstrasse*) but the bakery, hospital and laundries started 100 metres beyond the parade ground, to the right. The women's barracks were behind them, at the top of the slope.

Plaszow Camp memorial.

Turn left (south) at the T-junction, some 300 metres beyond the parade ground and after 150 metres you come to the camp memorial, a monument of four figures designed by Witold Ceckiewicz and Ryszard Szczypczynski in 1964. It stands on the edge of the earthworks called *Hujowa Gorka* where hundreds were executed, out of sight of the main camp. Two smaller monuments close by remember the Jews murdered here and the Hungarian Jewish women incarcerated in the camp. The wooded area east of the memorial was where the rest of the workshops were.

The film set in Liban quarry.

In recent years, Krakow's Jewish Religious Community wanted to commemorate the site and Iaroslaw Zolciak led the debates. The Proxima design group won the architectural contest to create a memorial site, announced in March 2007. However, many did not want the burial grounds interfered with and nothing was done.

Heading back towards the gate, you can go in search of the Liban quarry, a huge overgrown excavation to the north of the camp. The penal kommando worked in the quarry but it also played an important part in the film *Schindler's List*. The scenes relating to Plaszow camp and Amon Göth were filmed there and parts of the decaying film set can still be seen. A path does follow the edge of the quarry but do not try to go down into it.

If you are feeling really adventurous, continue north past the quarry to the huge Krakus Mound. This man-made hillock was supposed to be the burial mound of legendary twelfth century Prince Krakus, who built Wawel Castle and gave Krakow its name. While it has nothing to do with Schindler's Krakow, it has the best views of the city.

The Home Army Museum

The museum is named after General Emil Fieldorf, codename Nil, the Army's deputy leader who was executed by the People's Republic of Poland in 1953. It opened in 2000 after the organizers had spent ten years collecting items. It is the only Polish underground museum in the country. It is at Wita Stwosza 12, on the east side of the main railway station and it opens Tuesday to Sunday, 11am to 6pm. Entrance is 13 zloty (7 for concession).

Contact on (+48) 12 410 07 70 and http://www.muzeum-ak.pl

The Jewish Quarter and Museum of Jewish Life

The Kazimierz district was the original Jewish quarter where many round-ups and other sad scenes occurred. The area once again has a Jewish community and there are restaurants offering traditional food. There is also the museum of Jewish life in the Old Synagogue. In the old prayer rooms there are displays about synagogue ceremonies,

Jewish holidays and festivals as well as displays on private and family life.

The museum opens Tuesday to Sunday from 9am to 4pm, November to March, (Fridays 10am and 5pm) and 9am to 5pm through the summer. It is free on Mondays but only open from 10am to 2pm. Tickets are 9 zloty (7 zloty concession) and 19 zloty for a family group; there is a 10 zloty charge for an English audio guide.

The museum of Jewish Life.

Index